D1555554

NUMBER TWENTY-TWO
The Walter Prescott Webb Memorial Lectures

Essays on
Liberty and Federalism

[THE WALTER PRESCOTT WEBB MEMORIAL LECTURES]

Essays on Liberty and Federalism

THE SHAPING OF THE U.S. CONSTITUTION

BY JOHN M. MURRIN, DAVID E. NARRETT,
RONALD L. HATZENBUEHLER,
MICHAEL KAMMEN

Introduction by PETER S. ONUF
Edited by DAVID E. NARRETT
and JOYCE S. GOLDBERG

Published for the University of Texas at Arlington by
Texas A&M University Press: College Station

The paper used in this book meets the minimum requirements
of the American National Standard for Permanence of Paper
for Printed Library Materials, Z39.48–1984. Binding materials
have been chosen for durability.

Library of Congress Cataloging-in-Publication Data

Essays on liberty and federalism : the shaping of the U.S.
    Constitution / by John M. Murrin . . . [et al.] ; introduction by
    Peter S. Onuf ; edited by David E. Narrett and Joyce S. Goldberg.
    p.   cm. — (The Walter Prescott Webb memorial lectures ; no.
    22)
    Bibliography: p.
    ISBN 0-89096-341-X :
    1. Liberty — History.   2. Federal government — United States —
History.   3. United States — Constitutional history.   I. Murrin,
John M.   II. Narrett, David E., 1951– .   III. Goldberg, Joyce S.,
1950– .   IV. Series: Walter Prescott Webb memorial lectures ; 22.
JC599.U5E87   1988
323.44'09 — dc19   88-2105
                                           CIP

Manufactured in the United States of America
First Edition

To the Memory of George Wolfskill

Contents

Preface

THE WALTER PRESCOTT WEBB MEMORIAL LECTURES, held at the University of Texas at Arlington on March 12, 1987, form the basis of this volume. For twenty-two years, the UTA history department has sponsored an annual lecture series dedicated to the memory of Texas' most celebrated historian, Walter Prescott Webb. The theme of the 1987 lectures, "Liberty and Federalism: The Shaping of the U.S. Constitution," examines major issues in the formation and development of American government, law, and political culture. This subject is especially appropriate as we celebrate the bicentennial of the U.S. Constitution.

The contributors to this volume include Michael Kammen and John M. Murrin, the two distinguished guest speakers at the 1987 lecture series; Ronald L. Hatzenbuehler, the winner of the 1987 C. B. Smith Prize for the best submitted essay on the 1987 lecture theme; and David E. Narrett, a UTA history professor and a 1987 Webb lecturer. An introduction to the volume is offered by Peter S. Onuf.

Michael Kammen is Newton C. Farr Professor of American History and Culture at Cornell University, where he has taught since 1965. He is the author of numerous books, including *A Machine That Would Go of Itself: The Constitution in American Culture* (1986); *Spheres of Liberty: Changing Perceptions of Liberty in American Culture* (1986); and *A Season of Youth: The American Revolution and the Historical Imagination* (1978). He was awarded the 1973 Pulitzer Prize in History for his *People of Paradox: An Inquiry Concerning the Origins of American Civilization.*

John M. Murrin, professor of history at Princeton University, is the author of numerous scholarly essays on early American history. He has co-edited two volumes: *Saints and Revolutionaries: Essays in Early American History* (1984) and *Colonial America: Essays in Political and Social Development,* 3rd ed. (1983).

Ronald L. Hatzenbuehler is professor of history at Idaho State

University, where he has taught since 1972. He is the author of *Congress Declares War: Rhetoric, Leadership, and Partisanship in the Early Republic* (1983).

David E. Narrett is assistant professor of history at the University of Texas at Arlington. He studied with Michael Kammen at Cornell University, where he received the Ph.D. in 1981. Before coming to UTA in 1984, he taught at Cornell, the University of Notre Dame, and Princeton University. He is currently writing a book on inheritance and family life in colonial New York.

Peter S. Onuf is professor of history at Southern Methodist University. He is the author of several essays and two books concerning the Revolutionary era: *The Origins of the Federal Republic: Jurisdictional Controversies in the United States, 1775–1787* (1983) and *Statehood and Union: A History of the Northwest Ordinance* (1987).

Joyce S. Goldberg, coeditor of this volume with David E. Narrett, is associate professor of history at the University of Texas at Arlington. She has taught diplomatic history at UTA since 1982 and is the author of *The Baltimore Affair* (1986).

On behalf of the UTA history department, the editors would like to thank several friends of the Webb lectures. Foremost among these is C. B. Smith, Sr., an Austin businessman whose ties to our university date back to the 1920s. His generosity in establishing the Webb Endowment Fund has made possible the publication of the lectures. We greatly appreciate Mr. Smith's continued support. We would also like to thank Jenkins and Virginia Garrett of Fort Worth, two loyal friends of UTA. In future years, the Webb lecture series will be assisted by the Rudolf Hermanns' Endowment for the Liberal Arts. Dr. Wendell Nedderman, president of the university, has been instrumental in obtaining this source of funding. We appreciate all his efforts on behalf of the lectures.

We offer a special thanks to two members of the UTA history department: Sandra Myres and Stanley Palmer. For years, Sandra has been the guiding force in organizing the lectures and overseeing their success. Stanley has assisted the lectures in many ways during his years as history department chairman between 1982 and 1987.

Finally, this year's volume is dedicated to the memory of George Wolfskill, professor emeritus of history at UTA, who died on August 4, 1987. George was a student of Walter Prescott Webb and received his doctorate from the University of Texas at Austin in 1952. After teaching there and at Baylor, he joined the faculty at UTA in 1959. His colleagues recognized him as one of the best teachers and leading scholars on campus. He was instrumental in establishing the Webb Lectures, presented two lectures over the years, and edited several volumes in the series. He is the author of three books: *Revolt of the Conservatives* (1962), *All But the People: Franklin Roosevelt and His Critics* (1969), and *Happy Days Are Here Again* (1974). At his death he was writing a book on the New Deal in the South. George Wolfskill will be greatly missed as a friend, colleague, and scholar.

DAVID E. NARRETT
JOYCE S. GOLDBERG

Essays on
Liberty and Federalism

PETER S. ONUF

Introduction: Historians and the Founding

EVERY GENERATION interprets not only the Constitution but also the story of its origins and drafting in a distinctive way. A review of historiography clearly reveals these generational biases: Progressive historians like Charles Beard, with their heightened sensitivity to the disproportionate role of the "interests" in contemporary America, advanced an "economic interpretation" of the Constitution; consensus historians of the post–World War II era, responding to Cold War imperatives, deemphasized class conflict and accorded a central place to Americans' devotion to liberty and the rule of law in defining the new nation's exceptional character.[1] It is much less clear how future historiographers will characterize the work of the present generation. This essay will attempt to identify some of its leading tendencies.

The direction of current scholarship is never easy to discern: practicing historians usually emphasize their differences from one another, denying any common purpose or conscious intention of recreating a "usable past." And because history-writing has tended to become more "scientific" and specialized in recent decades, historians have become increasingly detached from contemporary concerns. In fact, despite occasional exhortations not to forget the proverbial "general" reader, they prefer writing for each other. Notwithstanding this professional isolation, history-writing is not now – and never will be – an autonomous activity. Bicentennial celebrations help illuminate the complicated, often apparently remote, relationship between historians and the larger public. The present collection of essays, written at a time when public interest has spurred scholarly interest in our constitutional origins, offers an excellent opportunity to chart the emergence of broad new lines of interpretation.

I

Preliminary reports on current scholarship have not been enthu-siastic.[2] In contrast to the 1976 commemoration of the American Revo-lution, the bicentennial of the Constitution has not been able to ex-ploit broad preexisting scholarly interests. When Americans observed the bicentennial of the Declaration of Independence, colonial history was the most vital, dynamic subfield in American history; a wide range of important and influential projects had already been completed or were nearing completion. Indeed, the celebration probably had a salu-tary effect on historians, not only by challenging them to address a larger audience but also by focusing their research on historical change and reminding them of the crucial importance of "events."[3] Extensive research and reflection on community life, social structure, and de-mography were thus brought to bear on the story of revolutionary mo-bilization, war, and state-building. Although scholars were predict-ably disgusted by the crass vulgarity of public observances, they were afforded extensive opportunities to tell their own version of the inde-pendence movement and did so with confidence and conviction.

The bicentennial of the federal Constitution does not come at such a favorable moment in historical writing. Ironically, the founders have attracted little attention since the neo-Whig interpretation, par-ticularly in its most sophisticated "ideological" formulation, gained ascendancy. Although the study of popular mobilization in the Revo-lution enabled scholars to forge suggestive links between social and political history, the movement for national constitutional reform remained — and remains — radically divorced from the kind of "history" most historians are now most comfortable writing. Historians tell each other they need to know more about the origins of the "state" and of our liberal political culture. They have yet to achieve substan-tive results, however, in bringing these concerns to bear on the found-ing period.[4]

Part of the problem is that historians simply have not known what to make of the Constitution. Traditionally, given the prevailing period-ization, the ratification of the Constitution has been seen as the cul-minating moment in *colonial* history: for better or worse, the main features of the new regime were now in place. Whether or not writers endorsed the "critical period" argument or saw true ideological conflict over the Constitution, the inauguration of the new federal government seemed to tie up the loose ends of the early period. The neat resolution suggested by historical periodization thus reinforced the mythic — and therefore unproblematic — standing of the Constitution in the popular imagination.

New work on the Revolution has transformed our understanding of the period: new interpretations and new categories of evidence emerged as historians traced the fate of ordinary men and women, and related their experiences to the great public events in which they participated. But the close examination of the founders, their interests, ideas, and intentions, has not brought us appreciably closer to an understanding of their world. In some ways, emphasis on the select group at Philadelphia — and even on humbler participants in the state ratifying conventions — has simply dramatized the great distance between the politically active elite and the great mass of Americans, without clarifying the nature of elite power and authority. This apparent disparity between leaders and led accords with popular mythology. In variant accounts, it has immortal founders creating a regime in which mere mortals could govern themselves, or has great ideas or principles — like democracy and equality — working themselves out through the agency of would-be aristocrats and entrepreneurs who did not grasp the ultimate implications of their work.[5] But neither version can now inspire serious historical research: even granting the importance of the founders and the founding for the history of American political culture, the challenge of connecting them to the "real" history of revolutionary America remains daunting.

The contemporary political climate may also discourage serious scholarship on the Constitution. Yet, if the national bicentennial commission has failed to take a leading role in sponsoring research, support has been forthcoming from a wide variety of public and private sources. At this point, the absence of a clear agenda, or of the compelling interpretive and methodological questions that inspired controversy in the mid-1970s, has been a much more significant impediment to original research. The debate over "original intent" — that is, over judicial strategies for reading the text of the Constitution — has united historians in collective disbelief over the historical naivety of the legal community, but has also served to preempt more interesting controversies *among* historians.

It would be a mistake, however, to conclude that recent historiographical and ideological tendencies have precluded any significant rethinking of our constitutional origins during this bicentennial period. The difference from the revolutionary bicentennial is again worth stressing. Then, relevant fields of scholarship had reached a stage of maturity that encouraged "paradigm consolidation."[6] But the constitutional bicentennial finds historians and political scientists in a state of disarray, and without such a clear sense of what they are doing. These are precisely the conditions under which a major rethinking and recasting of a field are most likely to occur. Several related developments suggest that this is happening.

Most encouraging is the current boom in legal and constitutional history. The new legal historians have begun to connect the constitutional superstructure with the legal and political rules that governed everyday life and facilitated or impeded private and public enterprises. Although few of these scholars have yet ventured into the founding period, they have already provided important new perspectives on the origins of the American legal order. Their studies show how legal history relates to the history of ordinary persons — the great missing link in constitutional historiography.[7]

The prospects for reinterpretation are enhanced by the eclipse of the traditional periodization. Although, predictably, social historians have taken the lead in discarding the conventional temporal frameworks — notably in studies covering the 1750–1850 period — the blurring of the old boundary between "colonial" and "early national" history should promote the reconceptualization of political and constitutional development. This has already taken place in a series of important studies that have pursued revolutionary rhetoric and ideology into the nineteenth century and emphasize the controversial reception and interpretation of the Constitution.[8]

Finally, recent work on the constitutional reform movement points to fundamental realignments of the old narrative in line with the new periodization. It is clear that the compromises of interests and principles at the Philadelphia Convention were neither "miraculous" nor final, but were instead deeply problematic and ultimately divisive.[9] The main features of the new regime were not the inevitable result of earlier developments; indeed, when the convention met, the continuing existence of the union itself was in jeopardy. The framers may have succeeded in reconciling a wide variety of frequently hostile interests in favor of a stronger national government, but only at the cost of subsequent confusion and conflict.

II

What have we learned from recent work on the Constitution? John Murrin's essay addresses a surprisingly neglected topic in constitutional history, the origins of American federalism. His most striking suggestion is that the "invention" of federalism — by which he means not only the creation of a workable federal structure, but also the "conceptual breakthrough" that gave that structure legitimacy — was the framers' greatest achievement (p. 36).

Murrin's argument challenges the accepted wisdom. It is generally supposed that the founders rejected the authentic federalism of the Articles of Confederation and, as the Anti-Federalists charged, created an essentially "consolidated" national regime. The rise of American democracy has provided the great organizing theme of scholarship, and issues of representation and popular participation — not what are today called "intergovernmental relations"— have attracted the most attention. Characteristically, then, commentators credit James Madison and his allies with creating a unified nation in the form of an "extended republic," *not* a federal union.[10] Because the Anti-Federalists doubted that republican government could survive over such a large territory, they resisted all challenges to the sovereignty of the separate states. But Anti-Federalists defended the states in order to secure their liberties, not as an end in itself: once proponents of the new system had shown that their "remedies" were in fact "republican" and that a "more perfect union" would secure the "blessings of liberty," no *legitimate* grounds remained for supporting the pretensions of "sovereign" states. Ratification of the Constitution marked a complete break with the Confederation's ungainly and ineffective federal system. In the extended republic, this traditional account concludes, federalism would be redundant, the last resort of interested minorities that sought to thwart the democratic will of the whole people.

Recent work on early American politics has called deep-seated assumptions into question, however, and has prepared the way for a fresh look at what the founders actually accomplished. Spurred by J. R. Pole's seminal essay — and exhausted by a vast literature on colonial American voting — scholars began to reconsider what "democracy" meant in historical context.[11] A broad franchise was not alone sufficient to establish the "democratic" character of contemporaneous politics, nor could it be assumed that voters used their electoral power for recognizably "modern," instrumental purposes. Pole and other students of early American political culture historicized familiar concepts, relating apparently democratic practices to the imperatives of colonial social and political development.

The great contributions of the new historiography were to establish the transatlantic context of American political discourse while emphasizing the enormous gap between the ideas and assumptions of the eighteenth century and our own. Bernard Bailyn's brilliant study of the "ideological origins" of the Revolution illuminated the formerly obscure assumptions and impulses that drove Americans to radical measures. But the new "republican" historiography that Bailyn's work inspired continued to focus on the classic questions of representation and rights.[12] At best, the disintegration and collapse of the British empire provided a narrative framework for the widening debate over the momentous issues of representation and rights. Not coincidentally, the "republican synthesis" was least satisfactory in accounting for change. When and why did "republicanism" lose its power?

The most influential attempt to relate political and ideological change has been Gordon S. Wood's *Creation of the American Republic*.[13] By locating "the end of classical politics" in the period of the founding itself, Murrin suggests, Wood has made it possible to reconceptualize the history of federalism. Juxtaposing the republicanism of 1776 to the liberal ethos that became dominant after 1787, Wood gave the history of political ideas a dynamic character but generally avoided the Progressive tendency to relate all changes to the rise or fall of popular power. If Wood's broad interpretation now seems too schematic — "republicanism" survived after 1787 and "liberal" elements had been present long before that time — his analyses of the development of key concepts at the state level remain compelling.

Murrin's major contribution here is to show that the real climax of Wood's story is not a decisive change in basic American precepts about politics and society but rather the "invention" of a new concept of federalism that "was conceptually impossible before the 1780s" (p. 21). Essential to this epochal "invention" were new ideas about the sovereignty of the people and the nature of constitutional government that grew out of experiences in the states. However much the Federalists' use of the idea of "popular sovereignty" confused and subverted subsequent theorizing about politics in America — one of Wood's more controversial suggestions — its immediate effect was to justify a truly novel distribution of power between national and state governments. "Popular sovereignty," Murrin writes, enabled "Americans to decide to delegate some powers to one level of government, others to another level, and to insist that these powers were as full and ample as any that a just government could possess" (p. 36).

Murrin's ingenious reading of the debates at the Philadelphia Convention explains how local experiences were "nationalized" through "a generalized learning process among the delegates" (p. 37). Whatever their predilections, the framers came to realize that they would have to adapt "the revolutionary principles that had welled up from below since 1776" if they were to succeed (p. 39). The promulgation of the new Constitution led in turn to "the first grand public debate" on the nature of the union (p. 42).

That the future of the union was the primary concern in the convention and during the ratification controversy may seem obvious, but is too often neglected by scholars. No such debate had ever taken place before. Prior to independence the fixation on the classic questions of political theory and constitutional rights had precluded any serious efforts to conceptualize and perpetuate the federal structure of the British empire. And, as Jack N. Rakove shows, congressmen wasted little energy exploring federal issues when drafting the Articles of Confederation.[14] But Americans saw themselves confronting a new set of problems in 1787 and 1788: the future of republican government now apparently hinged on successfully defining the "federal boundary," not on developing an entirely new "science of politics."

How do we explain this "conceptual breakthrough"? Of course, many scholars would deny that there was such a breakthrough: they argue that the founders intended to create a unified national polity and that prudential concessions to states' rights did not compromise their essential vision.[15] Rather than clearly defining the federal boundary, concessions to the states only led to misunderstanding about the true character of the new regime and gave a spurious plausibility to secessionist arguments. But the "nationalist" interpretation underestimates the broad commitment of the founding generation — including "nationalists" like Madison — to the preservation of states' rights; it also misconstrues the nature of the "crisis of the union" that prompted the movement for constitutional reform.

Contemporaries recognized that the success of the campaign for the new Constitution was not preordained. Throughout late 1786 and early 1787 there was growing concern that the United States might soon break up into three or four separate unions; monarchist sentiment was spreading.[16] Nationalists, Rakove demonstrates, were driven to despair by their fruitless efforts to revise the Articles.[17] Unable to regulate commerce or enforce treaties, Congress could not guarantee the new nation's security at home or abroad.

The framers' greatest challenge was to achieve a balance between national and state governments that would preserve and strengthen both. In doing so, they had to overcome conceptual obstacles, notably in dividing what was traditionally thought to be indivisible — sovereign authority — while, at a more practical level, guaranteeing specific local and regional interests that a redistribution of power might jeopardize. The resulting debate centered on means, not ends: most politically active Americans were "federalists" in principle. They disagreed on how well the proposed Constitution would secure its announced goals. Few Anti-Federalists had anything good to say about the Confederation, except by way of contrast to the embryonic despotism they saw in the proposed system. None, as far as I know, saw any positive advantages in breaking up the union. Indeed, the most striking aspect of the grand debate over the union was its narrow scope. The federal Constitution preempted serious consideration of the radical alternatives — notably, separate confederacies or an American monarchy — that were seriously considered before the convention met. To an important extent, the very existence of the proposed Constitution — even before it was approved by the state conventions — helped to resolve the great crisis of the union that had brought the delegates to Philadelphia.

III

Although the new Constitution may have made a stronger union conceivable — and disunion inconceivable — many, perhaps even a majority of voters, had serious reservations about the document. David Narrett's excellent essay explores the broad spectrum of Anti-Federalist opposition in New York, a state that enjoyed significant advantages under existing arrangements. Representing the most radical extreme, Abraham Yates obdurately opposed any expansion of federal power. Like the nationalists who thought concessions to states' rights would cripple the new system, Yates resisted Murrin's "conceptual breakthrough": disunion was preferable to any significant erosion of New York's sovereignty. Significantly, however, Yates stayed away from the Poughkeepsie convention, leaving the moderate Melancton Smith to lead the opposition to ratification. Meanwhile, Governor George Clinton, the most important Anti-Federalist, pursued a circumspect course at the convention, confining his most serious arguments against the Constitution to the pseudonymous "Cato" letters.

Narrett succeeds admirably in reconstructing the Anti-Federalists' principled opposition to aspects of the new system. Their paramount concern was to preserve republican "liberty" and this depended, in turn, on preserving states' rights. But moderates like Smith — and perhaps even Clinton — were also committed to federal principles; they recognized that local rights and interests could be secure only under a more effective central government. For the many moderates on both sides of the ratification controversy, debate proceeded within a broad ideological consensus. There was sharp disagreement, of course, on the future outcome of specific constitutional provisions. Narrett shows that Anti-Federalists' concerns about inadequate representation and potentially dangerous tax powers, *not* their definition of "liberty," set them apart from their opponents. The changes they advocated to secure individual liberties and states' rights did not seriously alter the actual distribution of power under the new system.[18]

The outcome of the ratification controversy in New York is best explained by the rapidly changing political context. New Hampshire's accession gave the new government enough votes to go into operation, making it harder for opponents of the Constitution to press for changes. Faced with the choice of joining or rejecting the new union, moderates like Smith were bound to switch sides. Anti-Federalists' motivations were undoubtedly mixed, but whatever their doubts and premonitions few were prepared to sacrifice the advantages of union or were anxious to follow Yates into political exile. "Critics of the Constitution," Narrett concludes, "simply had to accept the demise of the Confederation if they were to exercise any degree of influence in national politics after 1789" (p. 79).

Narrett suggests that New York Federalists and Anti-Federalists appealed to distinctive constituencies: if New York City was a hotbed of nationalist sentiment, Clinton and his party could count on strong support upstate from the "agrarian interest." But it would be a mistake, Narrett adds, to reduce these differences into a simple struggle between the forces of "aristocracy" and "democracy." If this was, in fact, the great division in New York and throughout the country, Anti-Federalist leaders must be seen as incompetent dupes or class traitors; if national "consolidation" threatened to destroy the foundations of popular self-government, opponents betrayed their principles and their constituents when they capitulated to the new regime. But Narrett's Anti-Federalists, in their "zeal for liberty," were confronted with a more complex situation. That so many of them came to terms with the Constitution — some at Poughkeepsie, and others afterward — does not mean that their "zeal" gave way to crass political opportunism. The relationship between liberty and union, and the definitions of both, remained problematic and this is why the Constitution inspired so much controversy. Men of good faith could change their minds in response both to changing circumstances and to persuasive arguments.

IV

Thomas Jefferson changed his mind several times. Ronald Hatzenbuehler's analysis of Jefferson's response to American politics during these crucial years shows how one leading statesman's devotion to liberty could result in rapidly shifting, apparently inconsistent, positions on the Constitution. From his vantage point in Paris, where he was American minister, Jefferson minimized the seriousness of Shays's Rebellion, proclaiming — in one of his most famous aphorisms — that "a little rebellion now and then is a good thing." Hatzenbuehler suggests that the Virginian feared that those "who wanted a stronger central government—and perhaps the English king again—planned to use Shays's Rebellion as their justification for constitutional change" (p. 96). This, of course, is just what the Anti-Federalists subsequently charged, and it is not surprising that opponents of the Constitution in Virginia claimed Jefferson as an ally. But they were mistaken.

Although he did have misgivings about the document drafted at Philadelphia, Jefferson soon realized that his worst expectations were unjustified. First, the revival of monarchical sentiment that led Jefferson and many other commentators to fear for the future of republican government dissipated as the reform movement gained momentum. Although the future development of the proposed executive was unpredictable, only the most doctrinaire opponent could argue that he would exercise the powers of a king. Secondly, and perhaps more important, Jefferson and other moderates concluded that the proposed system did *not* jeopardize liberty in Virginia. Given the tenor of nationalist agitation *before* the Philadelphia Convention, Jefferson had good reason to be concerned about assaults on the states. But the framers were able to negotiate and secure the "federal boundary" to his evident satisfaction. Persuaded that the Constitution was not a stalking horse for the return of monarchy and that its federal aspects were not simply designed to disguise a "consolidated" national regime, Jefferson focused his criticism on the need for a bill of rights to protect individual liberties.

Jefferson scholars will find Hatzenbuehler's insistence on the American context of their hero's thoughts about "revolution" and on his lack of enthusiasm for revolutionary change in France most interesting and controversial. Students of the American founding will also benefit from this essay's revisionist perspective. Jefferson's peregrinations on the Constitution are too often supposed to reveal his distance from America, mental as well as physical. But Hatzenbuehler suggests persuasively that Jefferson was a keen and perceptive critic of American developments and that even his most radical pronouncements reflected his understanding of the contemporary political context.

We might go one step further and argue that Jefferson's changing attitude toward the amendment process also was not aberrant: many Americans, including nominally Anti-Federalist moderates, revised their views on the proper sequence of amendment and ratification.

Hatzenbuehler says Jefferson changed his mind so many times because of his awareness of the nation's "precarious financial situation" in Europe (p. 100). But, of course, this "situation" was hardly novel; what had changed for Jefferson, once his anxieties about the basic structure of the new regime were allayed, was that he was persuaded by Federalist arguments that the movement to defer ratification and call a second convention entailed unacceptable risks to the union.

Throughout the period of constitutional reform, Jefferson, the loyal Virginian, remained committed to the preservation of republican liberties in the states, while recognizing the need for a more effective union. It is now becoming clearer, thanks to Lance Banning's recent work, that Jefferson and Madison did not diverge fundamentally on these points.[19] Like his mentor, the "nationalist" Madison never lost sight of his state's essential interests and never intended that the powers of the central government exceed their "practicable sphere." The two friends' roles in the great story of constitutional reform were, of course, far different: Jefferson's first concern, as Hatzenbuehler indicates, was to protect liberty in Virginia. Madison, driven to distraction by the Henryite majority in the state legislature and convinced of the futility of further efforts to patch up the Confederation, was persuaded that a new and much stronger national government was the first order of business.

Events showed that the two positions were by no means incompatible. The apparent paradox is resolved once we understand that "the invention of federalism," the great achievement of 1787, was a triumph neither for radical nationalists nor for states' rights advocates. Madison and Jefferson, together with many moderates on both sides of the ratification question, were both part of an emergent, authentically federalist consensus.

V

The essays of Murrin, Narrett, and Hatzenbuehler all reflect and contribute importantly to recent trends in constitutional scholarship. Murrin's provocative reassessment of the history of American federalism helps illuminate the neglected "crisis of the union." Narrett's rehabilitation of the Anti-Federalists gives us a clearer sense of what was at stake — and what was not — during the ratification struggle. Hatzen-buehler's revisionist account of Jefferson's responses to the Constitu-tion shows how suddenly and radically the framers redirected the course of American politics. But not all problems were neatly resolved nor, Narrett reminds us, were all Anti-Federalists immediately placated. Indeed, these essays are most useful in pointing us toward chronic and characteristic dilemmas of American politics: the "federal boundary" would remain hotly contested, even after the Civil War, and basic con-cepts like "liberty" would be subject to contradictory definitions and applications.

What exactly did participants in the ratification debate mean by "liberty"? Michael Kammen's work has revealed the protean charac-ter of the concept in American constitutional history. In the eloquent essay that concludes this collection, he focuses particularly on "per-sonal liberty," demonstrating that Americans of the founding genera-tion could define that nebulous phrase in many ways. For instance, when Madison referred to "public and personal liberty" in *Federalist* 10, he probably meant to differentiate between "public liberty as *free-dom to* do something and personal liberty as *freedom from* some act of intervention or encroachment, particularly by government" (p. 107). Conceptions of this private freedom could in turn be grounded in William Blackstone's emphasis on unrestrained physical mobility or in a tradition of "Christian liberty" that justified "freedom of con-science" (p. 110). But no definitive conclusions about either definitions or sources are possible: scattered references to *personal* liberty in the writings of the founders "do not cohere into a pattern" (p. 112).

While the meaning of "personal liberty" was ambiguous — and would remain so — confusion was compounded by bitter partisan divi-sions over the potential dangers posed by state and national govern-ments. Madison and many of his fellow reformers saw the states' vio-lations of property rights as the most dangerous threats to the survival of liberty and republican government. Opponents of the Constitution disagreed: the creation of a powerful national government was most to be feared. Samuel Chase of Maryland echoed Narrett's New York-ers when he warned that the subversion of the states would prevent them from protecting the "*personal* liberty of the citizen"— whatever that meant (p. 112). The debate over the Constitution thus precipitated a searching, if necessarily inconclusive, examination of republican principles. With ratification of the Constitution and the Bill of Rights, however, controversy became more narrowly focused. Americans generally endorsed the new allocation of powers, but the precise location of the federal boundary and the precise definition of the individual rights that the Constitution supposedly secured remained controversial.

Kammen's essay is particularly useful in revealing the problematic character of crucial constitutional concepts, both at the founding and during subsequent generations. His intention is not simply to chart the twists and turns of doctrinal development. Of course, his account *does* underline the futility of attempting to recover the founders' "original intent": "personal liberty" is nowhere mentioned in the Constitution, and therefore its meaning cannot be "frozen into a singular form by virtue of inclusion in a sacred text" (p. 128). Nor, given the wide range of contemporaneous nuances and emphases, would the import of the phrase be obvious even if it had been inscribed in the document. But Kammen's scrupulous attention to the meanings of key words in their historical context does not make him a simple relativist. American constitutionalism is deeply embedded in the nation's political culture, and Kammen's conceptual genealogy reveals important continuities as well as changes. Certainly the lineaments of our own conception of personal liberty are recognizable in classic formulations antedating the founding.

Kammen shows that constitutional interpretation, narrowly understood, is carried forth within a much broader and deeper tradition of American constitutionalism. His essay is itself a worthy contribution to that tradition. There is no "more significant social and political agenda," he concludes, "than the ongoing clarification of what we mean by personal liberty in response to our growing concern for human happiness, dignity, and autonomy" (pp. 128–29). Our attempts to reach such an understanding will benefit immeasurably from the efforts of Kammen and the other authors in this volume to make sense out of the founding and its legacy.

NOTES

1. On the historiography, see Jack P. Greene, ed., *The Reinterpretation of the American Revolution* (New York: Harper & Row, 1968), 2–74, and Richard Beeman's introductory essay in Beeman, Stephen Botein, and Edward C. Carter II, eds., *Beyond*

Confederation: Origins of the Constitution and American National Identity (Chapel Hill: University of North Carolina Press, 1987), 3–19.

2. "'Cerebral' Celebration of the Constitution's Bicentennial Is Derided as an 'Intellectual Bust,'" *Chronicle of Higher Education*, 33, no. 25 (March 4, 1987): 6–8. For an exception to this trend, see Michael Kammen's recent books: *A Machine That Would Go of Itself: The Constitution in American Culture* (New York: Knopf, 1986) and *Spheres of Liberty: Changing Perceptions of Liberty in American Culture* (Madison: University of Wisconsin Press, 1986).

3. For a good discussion of the rise of colonial studies after World War II, see Jack P. Greene and J. R. Pole, eds., *Colonial British America: Essays in the New History of the Early Modern Era* (Baltimore: Johns Hopkins University Press, 1984), 1–17. Alfred F. Young, ed., *The American Revolution: Explorations in the History of American Radicalism* (DeKalb: Northern Illinois University Press, 1976), provides a good sample of some of the best new work on the Revolution. A widely admired book combining the new social history with the study of political and military mobilization is Robert A. Gross, *The Minutemen and Their World* (New York: Hill and Wang, 1976). James A. Henretta called for renewed attention to events and narrative structure in his "Social History as Lived and Written," *American Historical Review (AHR)*, 84 (1979): 1293–1322.

4. William E. Leuchtenburg, "The Pertinence of Political History, Reflections on the Significance of the State in America," *Journal of American History (JAH)*, 73 (1986): 585–600; Thomas Bender, "Making History Whole Again," *New York Times Book Review*, October 6, 1985, 1, 42–43; idem, "Wholes and Parts: The Need for Synthesis in American History," *JAH*, 73 (1986); 120–36.

5. A recent example of the latter is Charles L. Mee, Jr., *The Genius of the People* (New York: Harper & Row, 1987).

6. The terminology is taken from Thomas S. Kuhn, *The Structure of Scientific Revolutions*, 2nd ed. (Chicago: University of Chicago Press, 1962).

7. Relevant studies include William Nelson, *The Americanization of the Common Law: The Impact of Legal Change on Massachusetts Society, 1760–1830* (Cambridge, Mass.: Harvard University Press, 1975) and Morton J. Horwitz, *The Transformation of American Law, 1780–1860* (Cambridge, Mass.: Harvard University Press, 1977). For the prerevolutionary period, the work of John Phillip Reid is particularly valuable; two of three volumes in his *Constitutional History of the American Revolution, The Authority of Rights* and *The Authority to Tax* (Madison: University of Wisconsin Press, 1986 and 1987) have been published. The vast growth in the literature is apparent in Kermit Hall, *A Comprehensive Bibliography of American Constitutional and Legal History, 1896–1979*, 5 vols. (Millwood, N.Y.: Kraus International Publications, 1984).

8. Lance Banning, *The Jeffersonian Persuasion: Evolution of a Party Ideology* (Ithaca, N.Y.: Cornell University Press, 1978); Drew R. McCoy, *The Elusive Republic: Political Economy in Jeffersonian America* (Chapel Hill: University of North Carolina Press, 1980); John M. Murrin, "The Great Inversion, or Court versus Country: A Comparison of the Revolution Settlements in England (1688–1712) and America (1776–1816)," in J. G. A. Pocock, ed., *Three British Revolutions: 1641, 1688, 1776* (Princeton, N.J.: Princeton University Press, 1980).

9. On the most obvious example, see Paul Finkelman, "Slavery and the Constitutional Convention: Making a Covenant with Death," in Beeman et al., *Beyond Confederation*, 188–225.

10. For a good introduction to commentary on *Federalist* 10 and the "extended republic," see Albert Furtwangler, *The Authority of Publius: A Reading of the Federalist Papers* (Ithaca, N.Y.: Cornell University Press, 1984), 112–45. The most important contributions to the literature include Douglass Adair, "'That Politics May Be Reduced to a Science': David Hume, James Madison, and the Tenth Federalist," in H. Trevor Colbourn, ed., *Fame and the Founding Fathers: Essays by Douglass Adair* (New York: Norton, 1974), 93–106; Robert J. Morgan, "Madison's Theory of Representation in the Tenth Federalist," *Journal of Politics*, 37 (1974); 852–85; David F. Epstein, *The Political Theory of the Federalist* (Chicago: University of Chicago Press, 1984), 59–110.

11. Pole, "Historians and the Problems of Early American Democracy," *AHR*, 67 (1962); 626–46. See also Murrin's excellent historiographical essay, "Political Development," in Greene and Pole, *Colonial British America*, 408–56.

12. Bailyn, *The Ideological Origins of the American Revolution* (Cambridge, Mass.: Belknap Press, 1967). The historiography is reviewed in Robert Shalhope, "Toward a Republican Synthesis: The Emergence of an Understanding of Republicanism in Early American Historiography," *William and Mary Quarterly (WMQ)*, 3rd ser., 29 (1972): 49–80, and Shalhope, "Republicanism and Early American Historiography," *WMQ*, 39 (1982): 334–56.

13. Wood, *The Creation of the American Republic, 1776–1787* (Chapel Hill: University of North Carolina Press, 1969). For recent commentary on Wood's book, see "*The Creation of the American Republic, 1776–1787:* A Symposium of Views and Reviews," *WMQ*, 44 (1987): 549–640, particularly Murrin's contribution, 597–601.

14. Jack N. Rakove, *The Beginnings of National Politics: An Interpretive History of the Continental Congress* (New York: Knopf, 1979): 183–91. For an important new interpretation of colonial constitutional history emphasizing federal issues, see Jack P. Greene, *Peripheries and Center: Constitutional Development in the Extended Polities of the British Empire and the United States, 1607–1788* (Athens: University of Georgia Press, 1986).

15. For vigorous statements of these views, see Richard B. Morris, "The Forging of the Union Reconsidered: A Historical Refutation of State Sovereignty over Seabeds," *Columbia Law Review*, 74 (1974): 1056–93, and idem, *The Forging of the Union, 1781–1789* (New York: Harper & Row, 1987), 52–79.

16. See the informative discussions in Merrill Jensen, John P. Kaminski, and Gaspare Saladino, eds., *The Documentary History of the Ratification of the Constitution*, 7 vols. to date (Madison: State Historical Society of Wisconsin, 1976–), 13:54–57 (disunion proposals) and 13:168–72 (the monarchical revival). Although little has been written about separate confederacies, sectional tensions are discussed in Joseph L. Davis, *Sectionalism in America Politics, 1774–1787* (Madison: University of Wisconsin Press, 1977); Peter S. Onuf, *The Origins of the Federal Republic, 1775–1787* (Philadelphia: University of Pennsylvania Press, 1983); and Drew R. McCoy, "James Madison and Visions of American Nationality in the Confederation Period: A Regional Perspective, in Beeman et al., *Beyond Confederation*, 226–58. On promonarchical sentiment, see Louise Burnham Dunbar, *A Study of Monarchical Tendencies in the United States from 1776 to 1801* (Urbana: University of Illinois Press, 1922). For a recent analysis of the "crisis of the union," see Onuf, "State Sovereignty and the Making of the Constitution," in Terence Ball and J. G. A. Pocock, eds., *Conceptual Change and the Constitution* (Lawrence: University Press of Kansas, 1988).

17. Rakove, "The Articles of Confederation," in Jack P. Greene, ed., *Encyclopedia of American Political History*, 3 vols. (New York: Scribner's, 1984), 1:83–91.

18. For an interpretation that emphasizes the elements of consensus in American politics, see William E. Nelson, "Reason and Compromise in the Establishment of the Federal Constitution, 1787–1801," *WMQ*, 44 (1987): 458–84, esp. 477–83.

19. Banning, "The Practicable Sphere of a Republic: James Madison, the Constitutional Convention, and the Emergence of Revolutionary Federalism," Beeman et al., *Beyond Confederation*, 162–87.

1787:
The Invention of American Federalism

AT ONE POINT in the Vietnam war, the Massachusetts General Court got fed up with United States policy and decided to intervene. In effect, it nullified the federal draft. Back in 1832, when South Carolina nullified the tariff, the result was a huge national crisis, talk of civil war, and finally one of the major sectional compromises. Out of the controversy came for the first time a coherent argument for the republic as a perpetual union. Daniel Webster, Andrew Jackson, John Quincy Adams, James Madison, Edward Livingston, and others all contributed to this increasingly powerful idea, a notion scarcely even contemplated by the founding generation. From this crisis also emerged a rival vision among some South Carolina and Virginia politicians and writers, a yearning for a separate and independent southern nation. Both convictions would gain momentum until they finally collided in the secession crisis of 1860–61 and the Civil War that it generated. By contrast, the Massachusetts nullification crisis of our time lasted only a brief period while the Justice Department found a court that would declare the action unconstitutional. Massachusetts accepted this result. No doubt the legislature never intended anything more than an angry gesture against the war, and that is exactly what it accomplished.[1]

This half-comic incident would hardly matter today except that it suggests something important about government in the United States. In our federal system, most of the boundaries between national and state power are well understood. Even where they remain hazy, the nation possesses well-established mechanisms, judicial and political, for settling such problems without resort to violence. The Reagan administration's Attorney General Edwin Meese would like to revive the early Jeffersonian doctrine that each branch of the government must decide for itself what it considers constitutional and unconstitutional.

As John Marshall's critics often argued, the Supreme Court cannot claim to be the final arbiter. A century and a half ago, this debate had an enormous impact on the political and legal system of the country. Today the effect is much less portentous. Not even the attorney general can alter quickly the institutional habits of courts and lawyers, nearly all of whom have been educated in the Marshall tradition. Part of the historical significance of the Meese doctrine is that, so far at least, it has *not* generated a crisis.[2]

From 1789 to 1861 disputes over what we might call the federal boundary occurred often, were regularly accompanied by threats of nullification or secession, and finally did lead to civil war. What most Americans do not realize is that this pattern is much older than the Constitution. The search for an adequate federal system, defined loosely here as a reasonably consistent and mutually satisfactory division of powers between a central government and individual colonies, provinces, or states, began in the seventeenth century. Before 1787 this process went through three principal stages. Each ended in failure. The old British empire, as it took shape between the 1650s and the 1690s, was really a functioning federal system without a sustaining federal ideology. The British government in effect abandoned the series of political compromises that had made it work and tried instead after 1763 to create a much more centralized empire. Colonial resistance to these demands led to war by 1775 and to a third phase in the history of North American federalism, this one dominated by the Continental Congress and the Articles of Confederation in which centralization yielded to state sovereignty. A compelling ideology of federalism took hold only with the Philadelphia Convention, the ratification struggle, the organization of the new government, the accession of North Carolina and Rhode Island to the Union, and the drafting and ratification of the Bill of Rights between 1789 and 1791. Even then, as the Civil War would demonstrate, the republic took another century to generate adequate institutional structures to sustain this new federal idea.

Today we take for granted the kind of federal system announced in 1787–91. Nobody at the time could. The federalism of the Constitution was conceptually impossible before the 1780s. To understand why, we must examine the earlier attempts to find an acceptable boundary between central and local power. Only then can we recognize 1787 as a supreme moment of political invention or innovation, a revolutionary act that permitted the Constitution to succeed after three prior arrangements had failed.

THE BRITISH EMPIRE

The improvised system of the British empire came close to establishing a workable boundary between localism and the obvious needs of a central state. In the early years the demands of crown and Parliament provoked frequent resistance in the North American and West Indian colonies. By the 1750s the settlers seemed happier with imperial arrangements than the British were.

The institutional structure of the empire took shape between 1650 and the late 1690s. The Navigation Acts, the customs service, the vice-admiralty courts, and the basic components of royal government all appeared in those years. The architects of the system, however, never thought of themselves as creating a federal division of authority. Sovereignty, they assumed, must reside in the government of England (or, after the union of the English and Scottish parliaments in 1707, the government of Great Britain), even if crown and Parliament frequently disputed their own respective spheres.

Nevertheless the central state did limit itself in two ways. It restricted its fiscal responsibilities by insisting that each colony must pay the costs of its own internal government. Exactly what this responsibility meant varied from one colony to another. More importantly, it forced the crown to negotiate this policy with the embodiments of local autonomy, the colonial assemblies. Naturally the crown preferred to keep its prerogatives as broad as possible, whereas settlers tried repeatedly to narrow them in keeping with eighteenth-century metropolitan practice. But in all royal colonies after the Glorious Revolution of 1688–89, crown officials eventually realized that they had to work through the legitimate assemblies or see their weakness publicly exposed. Successful governors, whether through persuasion or influence, made imperial policy attractive enough to assemblymen to win majority support most of the time.[3]

The second limit was also self-imposed, but it was less a matter of policy than of the structural tendencies of the entire British political system. Parliament's interest in the colonies rarely strayed beyond its concern for imperial trade. Because colonial commerce was overwhelmingly oceanic, parliamentary statutes affecting North America nearly always took the form of regulations of seaborne traffic. The classic examples were, of course, the seventeenth-century Navigation Acts. In effect, the British empire gave wide latitude to the individual politics of particular colonies but imposed much greater uniformity on imperial trade. If this division of responsibility seems natural and even inevitable, it should not. The Spanish empire, for example, kept very close watch on the political systems of individual colonies but lost control of their trade, of which perhaps 90 percent was smuggled by the mid-eighteenth century.[4]

When Charles II took charge of his tiny empire in 1660, England was a minor power on the fringe of the European world. A century later, especially with the defeat of France in North America and India and also on the high seas, Great Britain emerged as the greatest global colossus that humankind had yet seen. For all of the inefficiencies of the imperial system, it outperformed its rivals by a wide margin.

It did some things quite well. By the early eighteenth century, Parliament established effective British control over the commerce of the American and West Indian provinces. Colonial trade, which had been dominated by the Dutch in the 1650s, now traveled in British ships under British skippers who commanded predominantly British crews. So routine did this expectation become that when, for example, a French vessel docked at New York City in purported distress in the 1730s, the scandal entertained newspaper readers for weeks.[5] Likewise the major colonial staple crops — sugar, tobacco, and rice — went where they were supposed to go, that is, to Britain first and then to the continent of Europe. The main exception to this pattern was authorized by Parliament, which in 1729 permitted rice growers to export directly to southern Europe. Finally, the colonists got a huge majority of their imports from or through Great Britain. Smuggling of tea, brandy, and other products did occur, but the colonial market for British goods grew more rapidly over the entire period than did any other outlet. After 1740 it expanded faster than did the population of the colonies, which routinely doubled every generation.[6]

Other oceanic policies were less successful. The Molasses Act of 1733 tried to give West Indian planters monopoly prices in New England markets for what was essentially a by-product of the sugar trade, even though the British islands could not produce enough molasses to meet Yankee needs for rum and a cheap sweetener. This policy probably opened the door to more smuggling than did anything else that Britain tried before independence.[7] Trading with the enemy in time of war also generated considerable outrage, although the practice was probably no worse in American than in British waters.[8] Very likely the illegal colonial consumption of European and East Asian imports did increase after about 1740, although the Dutch were probably more successful at sneaking tea into Scotland and northern England than into North America.[9] The economic importance of this trade will always be difficult to measure, but in America its political significance became quite large. Boston smugglers, for example, played a major role in organizing resistance to British policies after 1763. They also brought into the politics of the prerevolutionary decade an animosity toward the Royal Navy that they had been acquiring at least since the 1740s.[10]

The crown also achieved considerable success in asserting basic control over the politics of individual colonies. As late as 1678 Virginia remained the only royal colony on the mainland of North America. By the reign of George I (1714–27), royal government had clearly become the norm. Usually the first crown governor in a given province experienced a rude welcome. He brought with him customary prerogative expectations that were bound to clash with existing institutions, such as the assembly and structures of local government, both of which antedated royal control in nearly every province. Most of the early royal governors were soldiers whose short tempers exploded when they encountered systematic resistance. They soon learned that they could not get everything they demanded, and yet they seldom lost or surrendered powers that they had once exercised with real success.[11]

Most defeats for royal government involved the failure to assert a prerogative that had never been made good within a particular colony. Massachusetts never granted a permanent salary to any royal official and never attached a suspending clause to any piece of legislation, even though both devices were in common use in many other provinces. From the British perspective, a governor who battled for these concessions usually looked like a gallant defender of traditional prerogatives, even though the struggle could paralyze his administration and prevent more essential matters from going through. A governor who abandoned the contest seemed, by contrast, to have "surrendered" a prerogative even if no one had ever been able to exercise it and even if he secured practical political advantages by dropping the issue. Thus when Governor Jonathan Belcher gave up the demand for a permanent salary in exchange for a fixed annual grant to be voted before any other legislation was passed, he successfully depoliticized the whole issue and secured what no royal governor had ever had in Massachusetts before—a near guarantee of a permanent salary. But to many in London the symbolic concession was far more visible than was the tangible gain.[12]

In other words, royal government in America is no simple story of linear decline. The most effective governors came late in the colonial period, generally between the 1720s and 1750s, after informal boundaries of authority had been established and were reasonably well understood.

Thus Parliament controlled the sea, whereas the crown administered governments that established policies for the internal affairs of the colonies. Yet British authorities never conceptualized this division of power in federal terms beyond using the adjectives "external" and "internal" to suggest in a vague sort of way that two such spheres did in fact exist even if they had no standing in law. Parliament's occasional intrusion into internal colonial affairs displays this lack of awareness. In 1699 the Woolens Act regulated colonial manufacturing only by preventing its seaborne export, an enforcable policy. But the Hat Act of 1732 attempted, quite ineffectually, to regulate the number of apprentices a hatter could train, and the Iron Act of 1750 tried to limit the number of mills.

More revealing were the various White Pine Acts that sought to reduce the Royal Navy's dependence on foreign nations for masts and other naval stores by securing a source for these supplies within the empire. On the eve of independence, Britain finally won cooperation from New England lumberjacks and timber merchants by paying higher prices for mast trees. In other words, an intelligent appeal to voluntarism became quite successful. But earlier coercive efforts to achieve the same goal mostly had met frustration over the previous half-century. To London it had seemed a simple matter to give jurisdiction over colonial mast cases to a judge of vice-admiralty, whose court did not have to worry about the obstructive potential of a jury. But in practice such a judge, operating a day's ride inland, usually found that local officials would not honor his commands. Condemned lumber that he ordered to be secured for the king disappeared instead. In an era when most public functions were performed by unpaid officers, government by consent meant more than working through the assembly. It also involved eliciting the support of local magistrates, few of whom were eager to damage the major commercial activities of their own communities. Just because Parliament endowed someone with authority did not mean that he possessed real power. Even colonial armies could be raised only through voluntaristic methods.[13]

Likewise royal governors, though stronger than ever in practice by mid-century, could always think of ways to increase their power. Few were satisfied with what they possessed. A genuine crisis, such as the early war years with France from about 1754 to 1757, could inundate London with panicky demands for strengthened prerogatives or direct parliamentary taxation, but Britain won the war through traditional appeals for voluntaristic cooperation. The settlers responded on an unprecedented scale and were quite proud of their role in the great imperial victory. This pattern intensified their inclination to idealize what they regarded as the status quo at a moment when metropolitan authorities were becoming ever more sympathetic to reformist pressures.[14]

THE EMPIRE: REFORM AND COLLAPSE

For what seemed to them the best of reasons, the British tried to change this system after 1763. An agenda for reform had been accumulating at the Board of Trade since at least 1748, and the passing of the direct military threat from France seemed to provide an excellent opportunity to implement changes that had been discussed in some circles for years. The exploding national debt added real urgency to these concerns. It had doubled during the war, reaching nearly £130 million. Payment of the interest alone absorbed about 60 percent of the government's annual budget. New expenses could not be avoided, particularly the cost of garrisoning Canada, Florida, and the American West with about seventy-five hundred soldiers. Surely, reasoned the administration of George Grenville (1763–65), the colonists would be willing to pay a portion of these burdens. The Sugar Act of 1764 and the Stamp Act of 1765 overrode colonial objections and imposed direct parliamentary taxation. At no point, however, did Britain ask the North Americans to bear all of the costs of their own defense.

Grenville was trying to meet the needs, real and pressing needs, of the whole empire. The colonists replied that Britain could not sacrifice provincial rights in the process, real rights, sanctioned by more than a century of tradition. Imperial policy threatened the principle of no taxation without representation and, by expanding vice-admiralty jurisdiction in unprecedented ways, it also challenged the right to trial by jury. Colonial assemblies and pamphleteers eloquently protested both the Sugar Act and the Stamp Act. Crowd action nullified the Stamp Act by compelling distributors from South Carolina to New Hampshire to resign. Nullification of the Sugar Act proved impossible. Ideological protests did not prevent the duties from being collected.[15]

Both sides searched for arguments to explain what was happening and to justify what they were doing. The British relied upon parliamentary sovereignty as a last line of defense but denied that the principle threatened colonial rights. Administration spokesmen invoked virtual representation to vindicate the new taxes. Members of Parliament, they insisted, represented the whole empire and were certainly as solicitous of the interests of North America as they were of nonvoters in Great Britain. Grenville's defenders also denied that they harbored any long-term plans for undermining the viability of provincial governments. Defense was a paramount need that all should recognize and support.[16]

North Americans replied that virtual representation on an imperial scale was a sham. An M.P. could legitimately represent British nonvoters because he had to share the burdens that he imposed on them. But every tax inflicted on settlers meant reduced taxes for the British. The Grenville program did not reconcile imperial and colonial interests. It polarized them, as worried provincials pointed out. If the ministry desired a colonial revenue, most North Americans insisted with growing irritation, it should ask the assemblies to vote one.[17]

The British government resisted a system of requisitions because its deficiencies had long seemed obvious. Noncompliance by any one province had a way of spreading rapidly to others. Parliament had overcome this obstacle during the Great War for the Empire only by resorting to subsidies, first pegged at £200,000 per year, later reduced by a third. Specie-poor colonies could claim a share of this amount in direct proportion to their overall contributions to the war effort. Although the annual outlay under this policy was less than what Britain was willing to spend each year on colonial defense after 1763, the government never considered continuing this wartime emergency policy after the Peace of Paris. Given the implicit choice, the Grenville administration thought instinctively in coercive rather than voluntaristic terms.[18]

In effect, the British argued that, although ultimate power had to reside with king, lords, and commons, the settlers had no cause to worry about their traditional rights. North Americans, by contrast, groped for a federal definition of the empire. They tried to find a viable boundary between the power of Parliament and the sphere of their assemblies. Most of them distinguished between Parliament's power to legislate, which they found legitimate, and Parliament's power to tax, which they condemned. This argument left some measures difficult to classify. For example, it bestowed approval on the Molasses Act of 1733, which most New England merchants loathed, but it condemned the Sugar Act of 1764, which lost legitimacy by *lowering* the duties of 1733. Reduced duties meant revenue, not regulation. And even while conceding general legislative power to Parliament, some colonial spokesmen — usually without explaining exactly what they meant — excluded their "internal polity" from this sphere. As Maryland's Daniel Dulany put it, "by the powers vested in the inferior is the superior limited."[19]

Both sides rejected Benjamin Franklin's practical distinction between external and internal spheres of authority. This argument did indeed limit the principle of no taxation without consent, for it bestowed legitimacy on the Sugar Act and any other port duties that the British should decide to impose upon the settlers. Franklin did not consider this concession dangerous. Most excesses would be self-correcting. "But the sea is yours," he told the House of Commons in 1766; "you maintain, by your fleets, the saftey of navigation in it; and keep it clear of pirates; you may have therefore a natural and equitable right to some toll or duty on merchandizes carried through that part of your dominions, towards defraying the expence you are at in ships to maintain the safety of that carriage." If duties became too high, he explained, both traffic and revenues would fall, and Parliament would have to rectify its mistake. Quietly he also suggested a voluntaristic method of raising an internal revenue for defense through the organization of colonial loan offices on an imperial scale. Only those who wished would participate, and the government's income from interest payments would almost certainly exceed what the Stamp Act had promised to bring in.[20]

Not even the reforming administration of the Marquis of Rockingham (1765–66), which did repeal the Stamp Act, was ready to accept this limitation upon the formal sovereignty of Parliament. The price of repeal became passage of the Declaratory Act, which affirmed a sweeping parliamentary supremacy that Rockingham hoped his government would never have to exercise.[21]

Franklin, with his extensive experience on both sides of the Atlantic, understood better than any other contemporary how the empire actually worked, but he could not find a way to show either side how to legitimate the political status quo. Neither common law nor the main schools of political theory ratified his distinction between external and internal spheres, even though he correctly understood that this line defined the power axis of the empire, the boundary between what Parliament could do without active colonial consent and what could be accomplished only with the cooperation of the settlers. Although in the early 1760s he had quite expected to spend his retirement years in Britain, his inability to make political headway with government officials drove him into the radical colonial camp in the decade after 1765.[22]

On a larger scale, Franklin's failure became that of the empire. It collapsed because its federal reality could find no theoretical legitimacy. The external-internal dichotomy kept reappearing, but neither side could handle adequately the disjunctions exposed by thinking of it in other terms. Parliament could indeed collect duties from colonial commerce. Through the Revenue Act of 1766, the Rockingham government again lowered the molasses duty, this time from three pence per gallon to one penny, and imposed it on both British and foreign molasses. Even though the quest for revenue thus triumphed over any pretense of regulating trade, colonial merchants found the measure far preferable to any other policy that the ministry had adopted toward molasses since 1733. Merchant compliance, in turn, worried committed colonial patriots, who finally took a stand against the Townshend Revenue Act of 1767. By imposing antimercantilistic duties on direct imports from Britain that could not be legally obtained from other sources, it seemed designed only to establish a precedent for general parliamentary taxation. Resistance was divisive and incomplete, and it secured only a token concession. The new ministry of Lord North (1770–82) repealed the duties on nonremunerative items but kept the real money-maker, the tax on tea. This gesture broke the nonimportation agreements and exposed the gap between colonial moderates and radicals, but it also drained colonial confidence in British justice.[23]

The same fault line emerged during the crisis of 1773–75. In response to the Boston Tea Party, the North ministry drafted and ruthlessly enforced the Boston Port Act, which closed the city to seaborne trade until the destroyed tea was paid for. This external measure was well within the capabilities of the Royal Navy. Britain could and did shut Boston down. The effort meant another political crisis, however. Publication of the act led directly to the summoning of the First Continental Congress and the organization of massive intercolonial resistance. The other important measure of 1774 was, like the earlier Stamp Act, nullified. The Massachusetts Government Act attempted to reorganize the province in several major ways, but the colonists refused to accept it and continued to function as best they could under the royal charter of 1691.

This resistance led directly to war. The fighting began at Lexington and Concord when General Sir Thomas Gage marched a small army westward from Boston to enforce the Massachusetts Government Act. Only by levying war on the settlers could Parliament exercise direct power in the internal affairs of North America without the consent of the colonists. War is not government. The British empire collapsed because neither side could explain adequately what it could and could not do.[24]

These crises were a painful experience for nearly all participants. The British never consciously tried to create a tyranny in North America. The colonists were not trying to destroy the empire. From Lord North to Samuel Adams, everyone hoped to find some arrangement that would guarantee imperial strength and provincial rights. Far more energy, intellectual and political, went into formulating plans to salvage the empire than into devising a new American union.

Several dozen such plans survive, the most famous emanating from William Pitt (Earl of Chatham), Edmund Burke, David Hartley, Lord North, and Lord Drummond on the British side, and from William Smith of New York, Joseph Galloway of Pennsylvania, and Franklin on the American side. Burke's appeal was the most eloquent, but its call for a return to 1763 could have worked only by somehow also restoring the mutual trust that had since vanished. He made no formal concessions to federalism but defended parliamentary sovereignty coupled with a promise not to use it. Chatham and Galloway drafted the most imaginative schemes, each with genuine federal elements, but neither could muster a majority on his side of the ocean.

Only North's plan became law. It embodied a parliamentary promise to use requisitions instead of direct taxes, provided the colonies paid what was demanded of them. In 1764, couched as a reward for colonies with a strong war record and a punishment for those that had done little, such a policy just might have succeeded. Effective resistance would have required the most loyal colonies to rally behind the least. By 1775 North's proposal had no chance whatever. It too relied on a mutual confidence that no longer existed.[25]

As the empire disintegrated in self-destructive war, the colonists finally had to ask themselves what an adequate North American union might be. In 1775 no one knew the answer to that question.

THE FIRST AMERICAN UNION

North America's first federal experiment, government under the Continental Congress and later the Articles of Confederation, also failed. The British empire collapsed because it tried to meet common needs by sacrificing provincial rights. Congress reversed these priorities. It protected local rights so absolutely that it never acquired adequate power to address general needs. This issue involves more complexities than I can discuss here, but several aspects of the problem do merit examination.

Why, for instance, did Congress have any power at all? It was strong enough to raise an army and fight an eight-year war, even if it could not command the resources to press the struggle efficiently. Why did Americans obey this improvised gathering of colonial gentlemen, most of whom did not even know one another before they all gathered in Congress?

The legitimacy of Congress derived from the struggle with Britain. America's root quarrel lay far more with Parliament than with the crown, but in 1774 royal officials saw no alternative but to enforce parliamentary measures. As the structures of royal government disintegrated under these pressures, Congress emerged as the new focus of legitimacy.

Although we usually think of Congress as a weak legislature compared with its parliamentary predecessor and its own post-1789 successor, we probably ought to abandon this conceptualization entirely, at least for the early years of the Revolutionary War. Congress was not a legislature. It was a plural executive. It imitated not Parliament, but the king. It inherited the role of the imperial crown. In closed sessions, it created and commanded an army and navy, established diplomatic relations with foreign states, printed money, issued requisitions, took charge of the post office, and decided questions of legitimacy within the states. All these functions belonged to the crown before 1774. Congress did not pass laws, levy taxes, or regulate trade — functions that Parliament had claimed within the empire. Nor did it attempt to exercise all the powers of the imperial crown. It did not try to appoint state governors and judges, veto state laws, or hear routine judicial appeals. These regal functions devolved upon the states instead, as did the general legislative powers of Parliament.[26]

Time muddied the clarity of this distinction between executive and parliamentary roles. The need for efficiency during the war crisis of 1779–81, when British armies overran most of the deep South, prompted Congress to create its own executive departments of finance, foreign affairs, and war, each under an individual minister. As this process took hold, Congress had to appear more as a weak legislature directing executive departments than as an executive body itself. But for all its difficulties, it encountered little public criticism. The most eloquent complaints came from within, from men exasperated with the "imbecility" of a system they could not get to work properly.[27]

Congress grew weaker for other reasons as well. In the environment of 1774–75, when the legitimacy of each colonial government was very much in question, Congress acquired real power by arbitrating these disputes or sanctioning the overthrow of an insufficiently patriot regime, as in Pennsylvania. But as the states went through their own process of constitution-making between 1776 and 1780, they acquired a kind of legitimacy that Congress did not have, and they also had antiquity on their side. They had a history. Congress was new, its powers an improvised response to revolutionary crisis and war. Even though Congress finished drafting the Articles of Confederation in November, 1777, the document was not finally ratified by all of the states until March 1, 1781. By then even its ardent backers believed that it needed structural amendment, at the very least a limited power to raise its own revenue.[28]

These Articles of Confederation and "perpetual union" between the thirteen states did become the first constitution for the new American nation. But their drafting and approval by the states had never really engaged the imagination of the public. Ten years of imperial crisis had called forth dozens of plans for imperial union and conciliation. The task of confederating the thirteen colonies did nothing of the kind. One brief proposal appeared in a Pennsylvania newspaper, and three others were laid before Congress, only one of which — the John Dickinson draft — had a sizable impact. Ordinary citizens scarcely debated confederation at all, not even during the prolonged ratification phase of the Articles. Only in Congress did the question get anything like an adequate airing, and then it had to compete with the war for attention, often without much success.

Any American union would have to combine large and growing states with small, more stagnant ones. The split between the two blocs emerged right away with the meeting of the First Continental Congress in September, 1774. Large states favored proportional representation according to population. Small states battled for state equality. Large state delegates were more likely than their opponents to advocate bestowing significant powers upon Congress. John Dickinson, who owned property in Pennsylvania and Delaware, and served both governments at various times during this period, resolved these questions mostly on small-state terms. He yielded on representation. Although most historians have read his draft as an effort to build a strong central government, he never proposed to give Congress power to tax or regulate trade. His careful enumeration of other powers was probably an effort to avoid a general grant of legislative authority. His list of delegated powers, though lengthy, was not controversial. It consisted overwhelmingly of activities that Congress had been conducting since it took charge of the war effort.[29]

If anyone questioned whether such a Congress would preside over a centralized or decentralized union, Thomas Burke of North Carolina ended all doubt when he introduced an amendment in 1777 that became Article Two of the completed text: "Each state retains its sovereignty, freedom, and independence, and every Power, Jurisdiction and right, which is not by this confederation expressly delegated to the United States in Congress assembled." States' rights thus triumphed over national aspirations.[30]

Within Congress, the text of the Articles had evolved mostly in response to small-state demands. Yet during the ratification process, large states quickly accepted the document. Small states prevented rapid action by demanding more concessions. The last four to ratify were Georgia, New Jersey, Delaware, and Maryland. Most of their spokesmen hoped to force large states to surrender their vast western land claims to Congress. New Jersey, tightly squeezed between the ports of Philadelphia and New York City, demanded that duties on trade go to Congress, not to the states.[31]

Despite its weaknesses, the Confederation accomplished a great deal. Above all, the United States won the war and negotiated an extremely favorable peace treaty. But by 1781 congressional finances were a jungle that threatened to swallow all intruders. Congress, after it stopped printing paper money in late 1779, discovered that requisitions were every bit as unreliable as Grenville had predicted in 1764–65. The war had pushed American voluntarism to its absolute limits and beyond. In the 1780s Congress requisitioned millions from the states but received payments that amounted only to a few hundred thousand dollars. Only one state, New Jersey, formally refused to comply with a requisition, and a congressional committee soon talked the legislature into rescinding its vote. But New Jersey never did comply.[32]

The desperate need for revenue prompted Congress to recommend amendment of the Articles of Confederation even before ratification was complete. But both the impost plan of 1781 and a similar proposal in 1783 failed to win the required unanimous ratification. Rhode Island blocked the first, and New York the second. Even European acceptance of America's victory over Britain could not dispel congressional gloom, nor could it quiet growing doubts about the viability of the young republic. Fleeing from protesting soldiers in Philadelphia, Congress moved to Princeton, New Jersey, in June, 1783, where the delegates joined students, various notables, and the local inhabitants in lavish celebration of the Fourth of July. The festivities calmed few anxieties.

Charles Thomson, secretary to Congress since 1774 and more familiar with its history than any other man alive, confided to his wife Hannah two days later that he saw "a dark cloud" hovering over America. "I confess I have great apprehensions for the union of the states," he explained, "& begin to fear that America will experience internal convulsions, and that the fabrick of her liberty will be stained with the blood of her sons." This concern punctuated his writings throughout the summer.[33]

The colonies had come together only to meet a common peril from Great Britain. Peace might well destroy the union, not perpetuate it. Those who had tried hardest to make Congress and the Articles of Confederation function smoothly were often the least confident of their ability to succeed.

THE CONSTITUTION OF 1787

Both the British and the Americans had confronted the federal problem. Each had failed. Both polarized the needs of the whole and the rights of the parts. As was just becoming evident by 1787, neither could get beyond conventional eighteenth-century notions of sovereignty, which a member of the House of Commons had once defined as the power limited by no power other than itself. The British and the Americans had agreed in treating sovereignty as an attribute of government. It followed for both that in a system with different levels of government, one or the other must be sovereign. The formal British argument assumed that king, lords, and commons possessed sufficient power to constitute a unitary state, even if in practice crown and Parliament were willing to concede wide latitude to subordinate colonies. The Americans explicitly lodged sovereignty in their states, which in the 1770s meant the state governments. They assumed that Congress would still be able to exercise sufficient power to keep the loose union of states together, at least for purposes of war and foreign policy.[34]

Americans needed a conceptual breakthrough to get around the dilemma posed by governmental sovereignty. Two developments nudged them in this direction. The more important was the constitutional revolution occurring at the state level from 1776 to 1780. The other was Princeton in the nation's service.

The early state constitutions, such as Virginia's, were drafted by bodies that also acted as ordinary legislatures. Although colonists had spent more than a decade trying to define firm limits for parliamentary power, their immediate answer to a sovereign Parliament seemed to be thirteen of their own. As several contemporaries pointed out, any body that can create a constitution can also repeal it. Despite well-intentioned homage to the principles of the separation of powers and the supremacy of the people over their rulers, American legislatures remained almost completely unchecked.

This pattern changed in states that experienced acute conflict over the drafting and acceptance of their constitutions, particularly in Pennsylvania, North Carolina, and Massachusetts. By the time that Massachusetts completed the adoption of its own constitution in 1780, Americans had found a way to institutionalize an idea that all had heard enunciated on many occasions but that no society had ever been able to convert into concrete and routine principles — the sovereignty of the people. The Massachusetts constitution was drafted by a special convention that performed no legislative function. It was ratified by the people, or at least by adult males, who voted on it article by article in their town meetings. Massachusetts announced, in short, that only the people, not government at any level, will be sovereign in the United States. This claim was more than a legal fiction. Or, if legal fiction it was, it has been the most important one in American history. No one yet drew the lesson, but popular sovereignty made it possible for Americans to decide to delegate some powers to one level of government, others to another level, and to insist that these powers were as full and ample as any that a just government could possess.[35]

This discovery took place at the Philadelphia Convention beginning in May, 1787, when graduates of the College of New Jersey displayed extraordinary initiative in drafting a new constitution. James Madison, class of 1771, set the tone and the principal line of debate as the primary author of the large-state or Virginia Plan, which his friend Governor Edmund Randolph introduced. It was countered by the small-state or New Jersey Plan, written by William Paterson, a 1763 graduate. In the struggle between the two blocs that continued well into July, Madison's classmate, Gunning Bedford, Jr., of Delaware, introduced the ultimate threat. "The Large States dare not dissolve the confederation," he proclaimed in what was, perhaps, the convention's most dramatic moment. "If they do the small ones will find some foreign ally of more honor and good faith, who will take them by the hand and do them justice." The Connecticut Compromise finally broke the impasse. One of its initiators was Oliver Ellsworth, class of 1766. Altogether, nine of the fifty-five delegates at the convention had attended Princeton, easily the highest ratio of any college in the land. They were sufficiently modest, however, to accept occasional advice from other quarters.[36]

As their prolonged struggle indicates, the delegates did not have these problems solved when they came to Philadelphia. Persuasive answers emerged only after four months of debate during a hot Philadelphia summer. Among themselves they largely recapitulated the process that had occurred over a four-year period at the state level. The Virginia Plan closely resembled a Virginia constitution for the entire United States. Like the Virginia constitution of 1776, it would have lodged sovereign power in a single legislature, a virtual Parliament for America. But the document that emerged in September resembled instead the Massachusetts constitution of 1780, particularly in its careful separation of powers. In making explicit provision for ratification by state conventions, the delegates drew directly on the idea of the sovereignty of the people. This result stemmed from no unique enlightenment provided by the Massachusetts delegation, whose prominence at the convention did not equal that of the Virginia, Pennsylvania, or even the Connecticut contingent. It arose, rather, from a generalized learning process among the delegates. Experiences and perspectives that had been local were becoming more widely shared. For the first time, an intense debate about the American union was under way, and it would spread throughout the land from Independence Hall in Philadelphia.

To reach that point the delegates had to innovate. Advocates of both the Virginia Plan and the New Jersey Plan flirted at times with what the French would soon call counterrevolutionary behavior. Alexander Hamilton did not even disguise his preference for the British Constitution or his wish to model America's central government as closely as possible upon British practices.[37] The degree of centralization that Madison favored at first marked a sharp repudiation of the localist passions of 1776.[38] Even though Paterson claimed to be doing no more than offering minimal changes to make the Articles of Confederation viable, his specific proposals might just as well have been borrowed from George Grenville and Lord North.

Article Two of the New Jersey Plan would have empowered Congress to impose "duties on all goods or merchandizes of foreign growth or manufacture" (an American equivalent of the Sugar and Townshend acts) and to raise revenue through "Stamps on paper, vellum or parchment" (a national Stamp Act). Congress would have to meet any greater needs through requisitions upon the states. If the states did not comply on schedule, Article Three empowered Congress to "devise and pass acts directing & authorizing the same." Article Six authorized "the federal Executive" to "call forth ye power of the Confederated States . . . to enforce and compel an obedience to such Acts" (Paterson's version of North's hated Conciliatory Proposition of 1775).[39]

Supporters of each proposal undoubtedly believed that they had a good case because Congress represented, at least indirectly ("virtually"?), American citizens in a way that Parliament never had. But many people considered it dangerous to give any central government the power to collect internal taxes except during a genuine emergency. Had Paterson's proposal ever gone into effect and had a small-state coalition ever pushed through a revenue package obnoxious to large states, the debate of 1765 would have revived at once.[40]

Of course neither Madison nor Paterson consciously used Grenville or North as models, but they reached similar conclusions in similar ways, by searching out what seemed to provide the most direct solution to the problems overwhelming the central government. The counterrevolutionary thrust of their proposals was situational, not premeditated, although the secrecy of the convention's proceedings undoubtedly permitted the delegates to be more frank about these sensitive questions than they would have been in a more public forum. Yet the delegates realized as they contemplated ideal ratification procedures that whatever they proposed would have to pass close public scrutiny. This necessity imposed discipline on their speculations and, in practice, ensured that the sovereignty of the people had to be more than a legal fiction if the proposed new government was ever to go into effect.

Thus a fairly conservative band of delegates found that it could avoid unworkable counterrevolutionary proposals only through revolutionary innovation. The large-state and small-state plans both led to dead ends. Only by borrowing from the revolutionary principles that had welled up from below since 1776 did the delegates have a chance of drafting a new kind of central government, potentially stronger than either of its predecessors, and yet resting on broadly shared popular convictions. The decision to create a new government and not just amend the Articles of Confederation was one such step. The determination to put the government into operation as soon as nine states ratified marked another step, for this proposal scrapped the "perpetual" union of the Articles, which required unanimous approval of all amendments.

The delegates were willing to destroy the union in order to save it. They had no guarantee that all thirteen states would approve their dramatically new form of government, and they knew it. Their decision was revolutionary but nonviolent. It was not a usurpation, for it could by its nature take effect only after a thorough public debate generated a favorable vote in at least two-thirds of the states. Popular ratification also served a more practical purpose. By avoiding both bicameral legislatures and the many state politicians reluctant to see their power diminished, it greatly increased the chances of approval. The Constitution had to win majority assent in only thirteen conventions, not twenty-four separate houses.[41]

As the delegates scattered from Philadelphia to their states to begin the fight for ratification, they brought with them a fully articulated argument for the federalism they had just invented. It was something new in the world, and they were proud of their creation. Madison bragged:

> Is it not the glory of the people of America, that whilst they have paid a decent regard to the opinions of former times and other nations, they have not suffered a blind veneration for antiquity, for custom, or for names, to overrule the suggestions of their own good sense, the knowledge of their own situation, and the lessons of their own experience? . . . Happily for

America, happily we trust for the whole human race, they pursued a new and more noble course. They accomplished a revolution which has no parallel in the annals of human society: They reared the fabrics of governments which have no model on the face of the globe.[42]

Madison had entered the Philadelphia Convention convinced that something had to be done to curb the "licentiousness" of state governments. He left persuaded that the nation could survive only by building upon and expanding the revolution in principles of government that the states had pioneered. In the United States, the people had become the constituent power. Madison still hoped, along with most of his colleagues, that in practice the Constitution would give everyday powers of governance to more distinguished men that those who ran the states in the 1780s, but he knew that the document had to be justified in terms validated by the popular revolution within the states. *The Federalist Papers* tried to meet this need.

Because the authors of the new government called themselves "Federalists," their annoyed opponents found themselves stuck with the label of "Anti-Federalists," even though the adjective "federal" always had implied decentralization of power. Anti-Federalists varied considerably in the degree of their opposition to the new Constitution, but virtually all of them agreed that a government as powerful as the one now proposed would be a menace to states' rights and individual liberties without the protection of a formal bill of rights, such as most states, led by Virginia, had incorporated into their constitutions. After five states had ratified, this issue became absolutely critical at the Massachusetts convention. Federalists won assent by a very narrow margin only by promising to submit a bill of rights for subsequent approval at the very earliest opportunity.

Many Anti-Federalists undoubtedly hoped that by confining the new government to powers specifically delegated, they could preserve the sovereignty of their state governments as embodied in Article Two of the Articles of Confederation. But as eventually expressed in the Tenth Amendment, this expectation found, at best, ambiguous fulfillment. By reserving all undelegated powers "to the States respectively, or to the people," the Bill of Rights injected the sovereignty of the people into the equation. Arguments for the sovereignty of state governments became almost impossible. The defense of states' rights had to rest ultimately on the sovereignty of their people, many of whom came to believe that through popular ratification they had created a new, national compact. Whenever the argument for states' rights veered toward state sovereignty, it had to be divisive. The Constitution in no sense guaranteed that the argument for an indestructible union would triumph, but it did make it possible for nationalists to build a plausible case.

As America's first grand debate on the union ran its course, a curious inversion emerged. At Philadelphia, large states had led the way in forging the new system, and small states had struggled to preserve something more closely resembling the Articles of Confederation. In the state ratification process, Rhode Island long remained implacably hostile and New Hampshire extremely suspicious of the new federalism, but otherwise small states ratified quickly and overwhelmingly. The Constitution seriously divided all the large states, which presumably would be the most conspicuous beneficiaries of the new order. Federalists won an indecently quick approval in Pennsylvania before their opponents had time to organize properly. But when ratification conventions met in Massachusetts, New York, Virginia, and North Carolina, an initial majority opposed the Constitution in each case. Only the pledge of a bill of rights, beginning in Massachusetts, secured approval. To the dismay of Anti-Federalists, Madison's bill of rights protected personal liberties, not states' rights.[43]

The overall pattern of constitutional change remains curious in the extreme. The Articles of Confederation, as we have seen, marked a triumph for the small states within Congress, but during the ratification process the large states accepted the document quickly, whereas small-state beneficiaries prevented rapid approval. The Constitution reversed this alignment. As every delegate at Philadelphia understood, the new order shifted power dramatically toward the large states. Yet most small states ratified at once, whereas every large state hesitated to accept the benefits it was offered.

Two considerations help to resolve this paradox. One is war. As long as the British provided a viable alternative to continental confederation, large states did not dare drive small states out of the union. But after 1783, small states had to ask whether they could survive on their own in the dangerous Atlantic world of the eighteenth century. Only Rhode Island, which owed its existence to its founders' defiant behavior and had two viable port cities at its disposal, could seriously contemplate a positive answer to this question. Other small states knew that the cession of western lands to the United States and the passage of the Northwest Ordinance by Congress — in New York while the convention sat in Philadelphia — had gone a long way toward soothing their deepest fears of a strong union.[44]

Large states, by contrast, could at least imagine an autonomous future. They, in particular, had to face another major consideration. The Constitution, precisely because it gave the central government direct power over individuals, correspondingly reduced the authority of all states. Big states had more prestige to lose than did little states, and they knew it. Their delegates in Congress had always sought a larger voice in the affairs of the nation. Their citizens had to decide how much power could safely reside in a distant capital. Within the Philadelphia Convention, only such small-state delegates as David Brearly and William Paterson had suggested that "all State distinctions must be abolished, the whole must be thrown into hotchpot, and when an equal division is made, then there may be fairly an equality of representation." The idea of attaching New Jersey or Delaware to a larger neighbor or two had occurred to many observers over the decades. Indeed the adamance of the small states derived in good measure from their fear of eventual obliteration. The large states had much prouder pasts. Their delegates knew that self-annihilation was not an option that constituents at home would tolerate.[45]

The American constitutional system was not just the creation of a few brilliant Federalists, although without the contributions of Madison, James Wilson, and their supporters it would never have been born at all. The completed system was a result, rather, of the first grand public debate on the union, a prolonged and searching inquiry into what the delegates of 1787 had accomplished. This controversy generated sufficient approval of the Constitution to launch the new government and guaranteed that it would soon have a bill of rights.

Although Federalists contemplated a central government of broad powers, both external and internal, the dynamics of American politics brought the Jeffersonian-Republicans to power by 1801, and they shared a much more limited vision of what the national government should do. As Jefferson declared in 1800:

The true theory of our constitution is surely the wisest & best, that the states are independent as to everything within themselves, & united as to everything respecting foreign nations. Let the general government be reduced to foreign concerns only, and let our affairs be disentangled from those of all other nations, except as to commerce, which the merchants will manage the better, the more they are left free to manage for themselves, and our general government may be reduced to a very simple organization, & a very unexpensive one; a few plain duties to be performed by a few servants.[46]

In effect, Jeffersonian constitutionalism tried to apply to the United States the old internal-external dichotomy that had characterized the British empire. One difference mattered greatly, however. Unlike Parliament, Congress did not control the sea. Not even independence could overcome that lack, as the second war with Britain would painfully demonstrate.

The result was not perfect, as virtually every Federalist was ready to concede and as the Civil War would demonstrate in the blood of more than six hundred thousand slain soldiers. But beyond any doubt it was something new in the world, and that something has survived even until now. Few generations can boast of comparable political achievements.[47]

NOTES

1. Kenneth M. Stampp, "The Concept of a Perpetual Union," in his *The Imperiled Union: Essays on the Background of the Civil War* (New York: Oxford University Press, 1980), 3–36; John McCardell, *The Idea of a Southern Nation: Southern Nationalists and Southern Nationalism, 1830–1860* (New York: Norton, 1979), esp. chap. 2. My account of the Vietnam draft incident rests mostly on memory, but for passage of the measure and the suicide of one of its sponsors, see *New York Times*, May 10, 1970, 32:3.

2. See, e.g., Thomas Jefferson's views of unconstitutionality in his letter to Abigail Adams, September 11, 1804, in Lester J. Cappon, ed., *The Adams-Jefferson Letters: The Complete Correspondence Between Thomas Jefferson and Abigail and John Adams* (Chapel Hill: University of North Carolina Press, 1959), 1:278–80.

3. For a recent study of this process, see Jack M. Sosin, *English America and Imperial Inconstancy: The Rise of Provincial Autonomy, 1696–1715* (Lincoln: University of Nebraska Press, 1985). For a concise example of how intelligent accommodation could increase the real strength of a royal regime, see David Alan Williams, "Anglo-Virginia Politics, 1690–1735," in Alison Gilbert Olson and Richard Maxwell Brown, eds., *Anglo-American Political Relations, 1675–1775* (New Brunswick, N.J.: Rutgers University Press, 1970), 76–91.

4. Though dated in some respects, Oliver M. Dickerson's *The Navigation Acts and the American Revolution* (Philadelphia: University of Pennsylvania Press, 1951) remains very perceptive in the distinctions it draws on this question. The best study yet made of how one influential group of colonists moved from noncompliance to compliance between 1650 and the early eighteenth century involves West Indian sugar planters. See Richard B. Sheridan, *Sugar and Slavery: An Economic History of the British West Indies, 1623–1775* (Baltimore: Johns Hopkins University Press, 1974), chap. 2–3.

5. For a sample of this material, see James Alexander, *A Brief Narrative of the Case and Trial of John Peter Zenger, Printer of the New York Weekly Journal*, ed. Stanley N. Katz (Cambridge, Mass.: Belknap Press, 1963), 118.

6. Ralph Davis, "English Foreign Trade, 1600–1700," *Economic History Review*, 2nd ser., 7 (1954–55): 150–66; idem, "English Foreign Trade, 1700–1774," *Economic History Review*, 2nd ser., 15 (1962–63): 285–303; John R. Pagan, "Dutch Maritime and Commercial Activity in Mid-Seventeenth-Century Virginia," *Virginia Magazine of History and Biography*, 90 (1982): 485–501. Compare also the population and import-export data in U.S. Bureau of the Census, *Historical Statistics of the United States, Colonial Times to 1970*, bicentennial ed. (Washington, D.C.: Government Printing Office, 1975), 2:1168, 1176–77. Note that in the Scottish series, all columns headed "Imports" should be labeled "Exports," and vice versa. Informed colonists were acutely aware of the importance of their growing commerce to British prosperity. See, e.g., Benjamin Franklin, *The Interest of Great Britain Considered with Regard to Her Colonies and the Acquisition of Canada and Guadaloupe* (London, 1760), in Leonard W. Labaree et al., eds., *The Papers of Benjamin Franklin* (New Haven, Conn.: Yale University Press, 1959–   ), 9:47–100, esp. 99. See also James A. Henretta, *The Evolution of American Society, 1700–1815: An Interdisciplinary Analysis* (Lexington, Mass.: Heath, 1973), chap. 2, esp. p. 73.

7. See John J. McCusker, Jr., "The Rum Trade and the Balance of Payments of the Thirteen Continental Colonies, 1650–1775" (Ph.D. diss., University of Pittsburgh, 1970), chap. 7–10.

8. The single best study remains Richard Pares, *War and Trade in the West Indies, 1739–1763*, new ed. (London: Cass, 1963).

9. The best studies involve tea. Benjamin W. Labaree, *The Boston Tea Party* (New York: Oxford University Press, 1964), 9, tries to estimate pre-Revolutionary tea consumption by working backward from statistics on coffee consumption in the 1790s. This computation gives smuggled tea nearly 80 percent of the North American market, but it rests on a false assumption. One cannot compare pounds of coffee with pounds of tea for this purpose, because tea produces several times as much beverage per ounce as coffee. The data for Great Britain are much stronger. See Hoh-cheung and Lorna M. Mui, "Smuggling and the British Tea Trade before 1784," *American Historical Review*, 74 (1968–69): 44–73.

10. John W. Tyler, *Smugglers and Patriots: Boston Merchants and the Advent of the American Revolution* (Boston: Northeastern University Press, 1986) is excellent. See also John Lax and William Pencak, "The Knowles Riot and the Crisis of the 1740's in Massachusetts," *Perspectives in American History*, 10 (1976): 163–214.

11. For a more complete discussion with fuller references to the extensive literature on this subject, see John M. Murrin, "Political Development," in Jack P. Greene and J. R. Pole, eds., *Colonial British America: Essays in the New History of the Early Modern Era* (Baltimore: Johns Hopkins University Press, 1984), 408–56.

12. For the larger context of this struggle within Massachusetts politics, see John M. Murrin, "Review Essay," *History and Theory*, 11 (1972): 226–75, esp. 261–64.

13. Dickerson, *Navigation Acts*, stresses the oceanic limits to parliamentary power. The best case study is Joseph J. Malone, *Pine Trees and Politics: The Naval Stores and Forest Policy in Colonial New England, 1691–1775* (Seattle: University of Washington Press, 1964). The most perceptive study of the voluntaristic ethic in the colonies is Fred Anderson, *A People's Army: Massachusetts Soldiers and Society in the Seven Years' War* (Chapel Hill: University of North Carolina Press, 1984).

14. See John M. Murrin, "The French and Indian War, the American Revolution, and the Counterfactual Hypothesis: Reflections on Lawrence Henry Gipson and John Shy," *Reviews in American History*, 1 (1973): 307–18. For an imaginative but controversial discussion of what the "status quo" meant by the early 1760s, see Robert W. Tucker and David C. Hendrickson, *The Fall of the First British Empire: Origins of the War of American Independence* (Baltimore: Johns Hopkins University Press, 1982), 65–209.

15. The classic account remains Edmund S. and Helen M. Morgan, *The Stamp Act Crisis: Prologue to Revolution* (Chapel Hill: University of North Carolina Press, 1953).

16. For the fullest contemporareous statement of the administration's position, see Thomas Whately, *The Regulations Lately Made Concerning the Colonies and the Taxes Imposed upon Them, Considered* (London, 1765).

17. See Edmund S. Morgan, "Colonial Ideas of Parliamentary Power, 1764–1766," *William and Mary Quarterly (WMQ)*, 3rd ser., 5 (1948): 311–41; Bernhard Knollenberg, *Origin of the American Revolution: 1759–1766* (New York: Macmillan, 1960), chap. 13, 17–21.

18. Lawrence Henry Gipson, *The British Empire before the American Revolution* (Caldwell, Idaho: Caxton Printers; New York: Knopf, 1936–72), 10:38–110, provides the fullest available discussion of wartime subsidies, but Gipson never assesses the effectiveness of the policy or even considers its potential as a precedent for postwar policy.

19. Daniel Dulany, *Considerations on the Property of Imposing Taxes in the British Colonies, for the Purpose of Raising a Revenue, by Act of Parliament* (Annapolis, 1765), in Bernard Bailyn, ed., *Pamphlets of the American Revolution, 1750–1776* (Cambridge, Mass.: Harvard University Press, 1965–), 1:619.

20. For Franklin's "Examination" before the House of Commons, see Labaree, ed., *Papers of Benjamin Franklin*, 13:124–62, esp. 144–45, 139; see also Franklin to Joseph Galloway, October 11, 1766, ibid., 447–50. For an analysis of grassroots resistance to internal taxes, see Thomas P. Slaughter, "The Tax Man Cometh: Ideological Opposition to Internal Taxes, 1760–1790," *WMQ*, 3rd ser., 41 (1984): 566–91.

21. Paul Langford, *The First Rockingham Administration, 1765–1766* (Oxford: Oxford University Press, 1973); P. D. G. Thomas, *British Politics and the Stamp Act Crisis: The First Phase of the American Revolution, 1763–1767* (Oxford: Clarendon Press, 1975); Robert J. Chaffin, "The Declaratory Act of 1766: A Reappraisal," *The Historian*, 37 (1974): 5–25.

22. Franklin's "Rules by Which a Great Empire May Be Reduced to a Small One" (September, 1773) and his "An Edict by the King of Prussia" (September, 1773) demonstrate how radical and disaffected he had become even before the final imperial crisis of 1774–76. See Labaree, ed., *Papers of Benjamin Franklin*, 20: 389–99, 413–18.

23. The best history of the Townshend crisis is Merrill Jensen, *The Founding of a Nation: A History of the American Revolution, 1763–1776* (New York: Oxford Univer-

sity Press, 1968), 186–372. Peter D. G. Thomas's *The Townshend Duties Crisis: The Second Phase of the American Revolution 1767–1773* (Oxford: Clarendon Press, 1987) appeared too late to use in the preparation of this essay.

24. David Ammerman, *In the Common Cause: American Response to the Coercive Acts of 1774* (Charlottesville: University Press of Virginia, 1974); John Shy, *Toward Lexington: The Role of the British Army in the Coming of the American Revolution* (Princeton, N.J.: Princeton University Press, 1965), esp. chap. 8–9.

25. For the major British plans, see William Cobbett, ed., *The Parliamentary History of England from the Earliest Period to the Year 1803* (London: Hansard, 1806–20), 18:478–538 (Burke); 198–205 (Chatham); 319–22, 334–35, 352–53 (North); and 552–71 (Hartley). On the colonial side, see Robert M. Calhoon, ed., "William Smith Jr.'s Alternative to the American Revolution," *WMQ*, 3rd ser., 22 (1965): 105–18; Julian P. Boyd, ed., *Anglo-American Union: Joseph Galloway's Plans to Preserve the British Empire* (Philadelphia: University of Pennsylvania Press, 1941); and Labaree, ed., *Papers of Benjamin Franklin*, 21:365–68, 408–11, and passim. The British plan that probably attracted the most attention in Congress was that of Thomas Lundin, Lord Drummond. See Milton M. Klein, ed., "Failure of a Mission: The Drummond Peace Proposal of 1775," *Huntington Library Quarterly*, 35 (1971–72): 343–80.

26. For this argument, see Jerrilyn Greene Marston, *King and Congress: The Transfer of Political Legitimacy, 1774–1776* (Princeton: N.J.: Princeton University Press, 1987).

27. Jennings B. Sanders, *Evolution of the Executive Departments of the Continental Congress, 1774–1789* (Chapel Hill: University of North Carolina Press, 1935); Arnold M. Pavlovsky, "'Between Hawk and Buzzard': Congress as Perceived by Its Members, 1775–1783," *Pennsylvania Magazine of History and Biography*, 101 (1977): 349–64.

28. The process can be followed in Merrill Jensen et al., eds., *The Documentary History of the Ratification of the Constitution* (Madison: State Historical Society of Wisconsin, 1976–), 1:78–137. The fullest narrative of the ratification struggle is still Merrill Jensen, *The Articles of Confederation: An Interpretation of the Social-Constitutional History of the American Revolution, 1774–1781* (Madison: University of Wisconsin Press, 1940).

29. The best recent account is Jack N. Rakove, *The Beginnings of National Politics: An Interpretive History of the Continental Congress* (New York: Knopf, 1979), chap. 7–8, although the author makes Dickinson much more of a centralizer than I would. For the split between large and small states as early as September, 1774, see Paul H. Smith et al., eds., *Letters of Delegates to Congress, 1774–1789* (Washington, D.C.: Government Printing Office, 1976), 1:30–31.

30. See Thomas Burke to Richard Caswell, April 29, 1977, in Smith et al., *Letters of Delegates*, 6:672.

31. Compare the ratifications of New Jersey, Delaware, and Maryland, in Jensen, ed., *Documentary History of the Ratification of the Constitution*, 1:128–37. See also Peter S. Onuf, *The Origins of the Federal Republic: Jurisdictional Controversies in the United States, 1775–1787* (Philadelphia: University of Pennsylvania Press, 1983).

32. See E. James Ferguson, *The Power of the Purse: A History of American Public Finance, 1776–1790* (Chapel Hill: University of North Carolina Press, 1961); Richard P. McCormick, *Experiment in Independence: New Jersey in the Critical Period, 1781–1789* (New Brunswick, N.J.: Rutgers University Press, 1950), 233–44.

33. Eugene R. Sheridan and John M. Murrin, eds., *Congress at Princeton, Being*

the *Letters of Charles Thomson to Hannah Thomson, June–October 1783* (Princeton, N.J.: Princeton University Press, 1985), 19. See also pp. 29–31.

34. On this point and many others, I am much endebted to Gordon S. Wood, *The Creation of the American Republic, 1776–1787* (Chapel Hill: University of North Carolina Press, 1969), see especially pp. 344–89 on sovereignty. Twelve scholars discuss the significance of this book, and Wood responds to their observations, in *WMQ*, 3rd ser., 44 (1987): 550–640.

35. For a brief but lucid discussion of this transformation, see Robert R. Palmer, *The Age of the Democratic Revolution: A Political History of Europe and America, 1760–1800* (Princeton, N.J.: Princeton University Press, 1959–64), vol. 1, chap. 8. For fuller accounts, see Willi Paul Adams, *The First American Constitutions: Republican Ideology and the Making of the State Constitutions in the Revolutionary Era* (Chapel Hill: University of North Carolina Press, 1980), and Elisha P. Douglass, *Rebels and Democrats: The Struggle for Equal Political Rights and Majority Rule during the American Revolution* (Chapel Hill: University of North Carolina Press, 1955). The constitution-making process is exceptionally well documented for Massachusetts. See Oscar and Mary F. Handlin, eds., *The Popular Sources of Political Authority: Documents on the Massachusetts Constitution of 1780* (Cambridge, Mass.: Belknap Press, 1966).

36. James McLachlan, *Princetonians, 1748–1768: A Biographical Dictionary* (Princeton, N.J.: Princeton University Press, 1976), 675; Richard A. Harrison, *Princetonians, 1769–1775: A Biographical Dictionary* (Princeton, N.J.: Princeton University Press, 1980), 548; Harrison, *Princetonians, 1776–1783: A Biographical Dictionary* (Princeton, N.J.: Princeton University Press, 1981), 465; Max Farrand, ed., *The Records of the Federal Convention of 1787,* rev. ed. (New Haven, Conn.: Yale University Press, 1937), 1:492.

37. For the Hamilton Plan, see Farrand, *Records,* 1:282–93.

38. For the Virginia Plan, see ibid., 20–23.

39. For the New Jersey Plan, see ibid., 242–45.

40. See esp. Slaughter, "The Tax Man Cometh."

41. For a slightly different reading, see Forrest McDonald, *Novus Ordo Seclorum: The Intellectual Origins of the Constitution* (Lawrence: University Press of Kansas, 1985), 279–81. McDonald's book is outstanding.

42. Jacob E. Cooke, ed., *The Federalist* (Middletown, Conn.: Wesleyan University Press, 1961), 88–89; Wood, *Creation of the American Republic,* chap. 12–13.

43. Robert A. Rutland, *The Birth of the Bill of Rights, 1776–1791* (Chapel Hill: University of North Carolina Press, 1955); Steven R. Boyd, *The Politics of Opposition: Antifederalists and the Acceptance of the Constitution* (Millwood, N.Y.: KTO Press, 1979); Herbert J. Storing, *What the Anti-Federalists Were For: The Political Thought of the Opponents of the Constitution* (Chicago: University of Chicago Press, 1981).

44. Onuf, *Origins of the Federal Republic;* Staughton Lynd, "The Compromise of 1787," *Political Science Quarterly,* 81 (1966): 225–50.

45. Farrand, *Records,* 1:176–79.

46. Jefferson to Gideon Granger, Aug. 13, 1800, in Merrill D. Peterson, ed., *Thomas Jefferson: Writings* (New York: Library of America, 1984), 1079.

47. See also John M. Murrin, "A Roof without Walls: The Dilemma of American National Identity," in Richard Beeman, Stephen Botein, and Edward C. Carter II, eds., *Beyond Confederation: Origins of the Constitution and American National Identity* (Chapel Hill: University of North Carolina Press, 1987), 333–48.

DAVID E. NARRETT

A Zeal for Liberty:
The Anti-Federalist Case against
the Constitution in New York

THE ANTI-FEDERALISTS viewed the Constitution as a fundamental threat to American liberty. From New Hampshire to Georgia, critics of the new federal system predicted the most dire consequences if the Constitution was ratified without amendment. National power would trample upon states' rights, a wealthy and corrupt elite would dominate the central government, and the people would lose control over their representatives. In short, the Anti-Federalists maintained that the Constitution threatened to undermine the republican principles of government established by the Revolution.[1] Richard Henry Lee, a leading Virginia Anti-Federalist, claimed to be shocked after his state ratified the Constitution: "Tis really astonishing that the same people who have just emerged from a long and cruel war in defense of liberty, should now agree to fix an elective despotism upon themselves and their posterity!"[2]

The protection of liberty was a constant theme during the political debate of 1788. Both Federalists and Anti-Federalists associated the concept of liberty with a series of rights guaranteeing personal and communal freedom. "Liberty" had both an active and a passive meaning—the right of individuals to govern themselves, and freedom

I wish to thank my co-editor, Joyce Goldberg, for her very useful criticism of this essay. Stephen Maizlish and Peter Onuf also offered helpful suggestions. Their assistance is much appreciated. While I was researching this essay at the New York Public Library, I had the good fortune of meeting Saul Cornell, a fellow student of Anti-Federalism. After we had shared ideas about Abraham Yates, Saul generously provided me with a copy of his insightful essay, "The Ironies of Bourgeois Radicalism: The Antifederalism of Abraham Yates." He subsequently presented this paper at a meeting of the New-York Historical Society in May, 1987.

from arbitrary or despotic power. The frequent use of the phrase "civil liberty" indicates that Americans did not equate liberty with license. As Michael Kammen has written, political thinkers in Anglo-American culture nearly always conceived of liberty as existing within the framework of law.[3] Individuals obtained certain liberties by their membership in society and by their acknowledgment of a sovereign authority over them. The idea of liberty was integrally related to the notion of personal freedom in an economic and physical sense. The "Federal Farmer," one of the most important Anti-Federalist writers, defined liberty as "security to enjoy the effects of our honest industry and labours, in a free and mild government, and personal security from all illegal restraints."[4]

Nearly all Federalists and Anti-Federalists viewed themselves as good Whigs — as men who were devoted to the idea of limited government and individual liberty. Once united in the struggle against Britain, they now divided over the question of how best to preserve liberty within a republican system of government. As proponents of a stronger central government, the Federalists emphasized the need to achieve a proper balance between liberty and authority. National unity depended upon the sacrifice of individual interests and states' rights to the general good.

Federalist spokesmen in the New York state ratifying convention criticized their opponents' single-minded defense of liberty. Richard Morris, a New York City delegate, accused the Anti-Federalists of being driven by a "zeal for liberty" to the detriment of the Union. Alexander Hamilton developed this idea more fully in a speech given shortly after Morris's remarks. He traced the public distrust of government to the struggle against tyranny during the Revolutionary War. Although the "zeal for liberty" had once been a necessary element in that contest, it had since become "predominant and excessive." Hamilton argued that a weak confederation of states could not guarantee the security of a republican form of government. A commitment to liberty would be dangerous without "*strength* and *stability* in the organization of our government, and *vigor* in its operations."[5]

Federalists saw their leading opponents as being either misguided idealists or scheming demagogues. Hamilton warned in *The Federalist* that high officials in state governments would be among the most formidable critics of the Constitution. These men would seek public support by presenting the desire for an efficient national government as a drive for despotism and hostility to liberty. Hamilton cautioned his readers that the greatest danger to liberty arose from politicians who paid "obsequious court to the people" for their own selfish purposes.[6]

The debate over liberty in 1788 necessarily raised a series of specific issues concerning national power, state sovereignty, and representative government. Historians have tended to analyze this controversy in terms established by the contending parties themselves. Scholars have criticized the Anti-Federalists, for example, by emphasizing either their ideological rigidity or their Machiavellianism. Cecelia Kenyon has characterized the critics of the Constitution as "men of little faith"— politicians whose excessive fear of governmental power led them to imagine conspiracies against liberty behind every nationalistic measure. Forrest McDonald has advanced the less charitable view of the Anti-Federalists as an alliance of "knaves and fools"— a coalition of self-seeking state politicians and their misguided followers. The difference in viewpoints between these two scholars can partly be attributed to their distinct approaches to the history of the Constitution. Kenyon has analyzed Anti-Federalist thought, whereas McDonald has focused upon the political and economic interests that influenced men's allegiance.[7] Both historians' arguments correspond to distinct aspects of the Federalist critique of their opponents.

The Anti-Federalists have, of course, suffered from no lack of admirers among professional historians. Scholars writing in the Progressive tradition have identified a democratic impulse behind Anti-Federalist rhetoric and conduct. Gordon Wood has pronounced leading critics of the Constitution to be "true champions of the most extreme kind of democratic and egalitarian politics expressed in the Revolutionary era." He has also described the Anti-Federalists, not the Founders, as "the real harbingers of the moral and political world we know — the liberal, democratic, commercially advanced world of individual pursuits of happiness."[8] Wood has emphasized the democratic nature of Anti-Federalist thought. Historians from Charles Beard to Edward Countryman have examined the social and economic bonds between Anti-Federalist politicians and their supporters. Although most scholars since the mid-1950s have either rejected or else modified Beard's specific economic categories, many historians continue to view the Anti-Federalists as spokesmen for the common people against an elite.[9]

The most persuasive versions of the Progressive interpretation acknowledge the complexity of American society during the era of the Constitution. The domestic politics of this period cannot be understood simply as a struggle between the rich and the poor, or the few and the many.[10] The interests of Anti-Federalist leaders should not, for example, be equated with their followers' concerns. Consider the case of three prominent New York Anti-Federalists: George Clinton, Melancton Smith, and Abraham Yates, Jr. Although these men strongly identified with the yeomanry, they often engaged in the same type of economic activities as their principal opponents — land speculation, the leasing of land to tenant farmers, or the ownership of government securities. The historian Alfred Young has characterized the popular Whigs' policies as furthering the "politics of opportunity," not the goal of social leveling.[11]

Anti-Federalist political ideology cannot easily be classified; it embodied several distinct tendencies in Revolutionary thought. Critics of the Constitution were conservative because they sought to preserve a federal system devoted to the protection of individual freedom and states' rights. As heirs to the radical Whig political tradition, they were often more concerned about checking the abuse of governmental power than in broadening the extent of popular participation in government. At the same time that they espoused conservative principles, they also challenged the existing social order by rejecting the idea of deference. Men were responsible for their own freedom. They should not depend upon a group of wealthy, educated leaders to protect their interests, even if those leaders exercised power in the name of the people. The Anti-Federalists expressed their zeal for liberty in terms that transcended their narrow interest as state politicians. They objected to the Constitution on the basis that it favored the interests of the "well-born" to the detriment of ordinary citizens.

Some Anti-Federalists conceived of a just government as achieving a balance between distinct interest groups. The "Federal Farmer" favored a system of representation in Congress that would enable "professional men, merchants, traders, farmers, mechanics, &c. to bring a just proportion of their best informed men into the legislature." Gordon Wood has interpreted this statement as an endorsement of 1980s-style pluralism.[12] The Anti-Federalists, however, generally rejected the notion that the public good could best be advanced by the pursuit of private interests. They favored an enhanced political role for the middle classes because they believed that this group was less inclined than either the wealthy or the poor to promote its self-interest at the expense of others. The "Federal Farmer," for example, argued that "men of middling property" were the most genuine friends of republicanism. He contrasted them with the "aristocrats" who threatened free government from above and the "levelers" who threatened it from below.[13]

The Anti-Federalists avidly sought the freeholders' votes for pragmatic as well as ideological reasons. They had to win the support of ordinary citizens if they were to limit the powers of the central government. The strength of republican values among the Anti-Federalists helps to explain the frequent discrepancy between their public pronouncements and their personal behavior. As much as the Federalists, they were apt to promote the ideal of civic virtue while seeking their own material advantage.

New York provides a good example for understanding the Anti-Federalist conception of liberty. The opponents of the Constitution received a greater degree of electoral support in New York than they obtained in any other state except Rhode Island. In the election of April, 1788, New York voters chose forty-six Anti-Federalists and only nineteen Federalists to the state convention that would pass judgment on the Constitution. Unfortunately for the majority party, the outcome of the political conflict in New York depended upon events outside the state. By the time that the New York convention convened in Poughkeepsie on June 17, eight states had already approved the Constitution. When New Hampshire and Virginia ratified the federal system in late June, the New York Anti-Federalists confronted a particularly troubling situation. They then had to accept the reality that ten states recognized the Constitution as the supreme law of the land. Although the New Yorkers wished to be included within the Union, they vowed not to ratify the Constitution unless they obtained some guarantees that the document would be amended. According to one complex Anti-Federalist proposal, the state convention would attach a lengthy list of amendments, including a bill of rights, to the act of ratification. New York would then recognize only a limited degree of federal authority until Congress called a new federal convention — a meeting of delegates from all the states to consider these recommendations for change.

The Poughkeepsie convention might easily have ended in stalemate had not some Anti-Federalists eventually dropped this demand after several weeks of debate. These delegates, led by Melancton Smith of Dutchess County, became convinced that Congress would not accept New York into the Union if the state restricted federal authority or reserved the right to withdraw from the national compact. They accepted the Federalists' argument that the failure to ratify would result in economic and political chaos, including the possible secession of pro-Federalist New York City and nearby areas from the northern part of the state. They therefore proposed to approve the Constitution "in full confidence," but not on the condition that a second constitutional convention would be called. Because twelve Anti-Federalists broke with their party and adopted this new position, the state convention ratified the Constitution on July 26 by the narrow margin of thirty to twenty-seven. As a concession to the Anti-Federalists, the act of ratification affirmed the importance of specific personal freedoms and states' rights; the instrument also included a lengthy list of amendments for the consideration of Congress. Finally, the delegates unanimously agreed to a circular letter addressed to the state governors for the purpose of promoting a general convention. The final form of ratification represented a victory for the Federalists, but it also expressed their opponents' legitimate concerns. The extent of the Anti-Federalist defeat became apparent only as the second convention movement collapsed the next year.[14]

Considering the political circumstances in July, 1788, it is not surprising that some New York Anti-Federalists decided to vote for ratification. Their action enabled New York to join a Union that was vital to the state's economic and political interests. It is more striking, however, that so many delegates refused to accept the Constitution even with the concessions offered by their political opponents. Most Anti-Federalists in both New York and other states put little faith in the opposition's pledge to promote amendments after the new national government took effect. This skepticism proved well founded; only a limited number of Anti-Federalist demands subsequently were incorporated into the Bill of Rights. The first ten amendments addressed the Anti-Federalist concern with individual liberty but imposed no significant restrictions upon the federal government's enumerated powers. It should be emphasized that five states—Massachusetts, South Carolina, New Hampshire, Virginia, and New York—successively ratified the Constitution in 1788 while proposing significant changes in that document. Two other states—North Carolina and Rhode Island —found the new federal system so objectionable that they initially refused to join it. They, too, adopted a series of amendments when they respectively ratified the Constitution in 1789 and 1790.[15]

New York Anti-Federalists agreed with their allies in other states that each branch of the proposed national government represented a threat to liberty. They also feared that the federal legislature, executive, and judiciary were too closely linked to check each other's powers effectively.[16] The Anti-Federalists recommended certain changes in all three branches; their most significant demands for governmental reform concerned Congress. The New York state convention adopted amendments that sought to restrict congressional control over federal elections, regulation of state militias, and establishment of federal courts. The convention also recommended that a two-thirds majority in Congress be necessary to raise or maintain an army in peacetime, to borrow money on the credit of the United States, and to declare war. Some of the most important Anti-Federalist amendments concerned representation and taxation—two core issues of the Revolution. The New York convention joined four other states in 1788 by proposing that the House of Representatives be made a more democratic body—that the number of representatives be increased in relation to population. New York alone that year approved two Anti-Federalist demands concerning the Senate—that the state legislatures be empowered to recall senators, and that rotation in office be mandatory in the Senate. Five state conventions, including that of New York, voted in 1788 to restrict the congressional power of taxation, particularly direct taxation of citizens.[17]

Some historians have viewed the Anti-Federalist proposal of amendments as evidence of their political moderation. William E. Nelson has argued that the vast majority of Anti-Federalists favored the goal of strengthening the powers of the central government. In his view, the political conflict over ratification was simply a dispute about finding the best means toward the same general ends.[18] This thesis has some merit, but it fails to appreciate the degree of Anti-Federalist discontent with the Constitution. Although most Anti-Federalists supported a more efficient federal system, they perceived the Constitution as an essentially nationalistic document that could destroy states' rights and individual liberty. Their criticism of centralized power was often astute despite their tendency to exaggerate the danger of tyranny itself. They could not assume in 1788 that the federal government would be circumspect in exercising its new constitutional powers.

It is important to recognize that the Anti-Federalists were a coalition of politicians who favored distinct solutions to the federal problem. Melancton Smith, Abraham Yates, Jr., and George Clinton were three of the most important Anti-Federalist leaders in New York. They also exemplify the range of Anti-Federalist opinion concerning the issues of representation and taxation. Each of these men promoted the principle of liberty in a distinct manner. As a moderate Anti-Federalist, Smith was willing to accept the new national government if it could be made both more responsive to state interests and more representative of the average freeholders. He was the most eloquent and outspoken Anti-Federalist delegate at the New York ratifying convention. His speeches at Poughkeepsie correspond closely to the essays of "Brutus" and the "Federal Farmer," two of the most sophisticated political theorists among all Anti-Federalists.[19]

Abraham Yates, Jr., was the most extreme opponent of the Constitution among leading New York politicians. He once boasted to Alexander Hamilton that "rather than to adopt the Constitution I would risk a government of Jew, Turk, or Infidle [sic]."[20] Because Yates was not a delegate to the state ratifying convention, he avoided any responsibility for bargaining with his political opponents. Writing as "Sidney," he devoted his considerable talents as a propagandist to criticizing the Constitution without offering any positive solution to the federal problem. His zeal for liberty was more important than his commitment to the Union.[21]

George Clinton's politics are not as easy to characterize as Yates's. As the governor of New York, he attempted to maintain a pose of nonpartisanship that belied his opposition to the Constitution. He was possibly the author of the "Cato" essays, a series of newspaper articles that viewed the Constitution primarily as a threat to state sovereignty.[22] Unlike either "Brutus" or Melancton Smith, the author of "Cato" devoted relatively little attention to criticizing the Constitution for not establishing a Congress that was representative of the middle classes. Clinton himself directed most of his speeches in the state ratifying convention to the issue of "consolidation," the creation of a national government. He maintained his reputation as a champion of state sovereignty by voting against ratification.

THE ISSUE OF REPRESENTATION

Nearly all American politicians assumed that a representative system of government was essential to the maintenance of liberty. "There can be no free government," the essayist "Brutus" wrote, "when the people are not possessed of the power of making the laws by which they are governed, either in their own persons, or by others substituted in their stead."[23]

The Anti-Federalists viewed the Constitution as violating the principle of representative government for several reasons. They argued that a system of popular representation could not be devised for such an extensive and diverse country as the United States. George Clinton maintained that the states were as different from each other as rival nations. Congressmen would therefore be unable to perform their duties as representatives because they would be "totally unacquainted with all those local circumstances of any particular state, which mark the proper objects of laws, and especially of taxation."[24] The essayist "Cato" developed a related point in explaining why a policy of centralization would be bound to violate liberty. He maintained that the national government would encounter resistance in particular locales if it attempted to legislate for all the states. Congress could then impose its will only through the use of force. The adoption of the Constitution in its original form would lead eventually to a despotic form of government dependent upon military coercion.[25]

New York Anti-Federalists confronted the same political dilemmas as their allies in other states. Most wished to enhance federal power while retaining state representation as the basis of the Union. John Lansing and Robert Yates had left the Philadelphia Convention rather than yield the rule of one state/one vote in Congress. George Clinton supported them. His objections to the Constitution began with that document's first words: "We the People of the United States." He declared in the New York ratifying convention that any truly federal system must recognize that the states are "equally free and independent . . . that they are to be considered as moral persons, having a will of their own and equal rights — that these rights are freedom, sovereignty, and independence."[26] Although Clinton expressed his zeal for states' rights in uncompromising terms, his opposition to the Constitution was not absolute. As a practical politician, he recognized that his party could most effectively resist the movement toward "consolidation" by controlling rather than by simply opposing the process of reform. The "Anti's" sought to amend the Constitution while generally rejecting that document's basic premise — that republican government could work on the national level.

Abraham Yates was even more extreme than Clinton in his advocacy of state sovereignty. He described the Articles of Confederation in 1786 as the best of all possible governments.[27] The federal government could exercise legitimate authority only as long as it acted as a council representing independent and sovereign states. Yates believed that state officials could not fulfill their duties if they were compelled to swear allegiance to the new federal Constitution. A man could not obey both the state legislature and Congress any more than he could serve two masters with competing interests. Although the state constitution was designed to safeguard liberty, the new national government would be one of "wanton oppression."[28]

While Clinton and Yates emphasized the danger of establishing a national legislature, other Anti-Federalists focused upon the organization of the proposed Congress. Melancton Smith charged that Congress, particularly the House, lacked a sufficient number of representatives to express public opinion. He claimed that sixty-five men could not represent adequately the interests of three million persons; one man could hardly speak for the concerns of thirty thousand. If Congress was to act as a national legislature, the ratio between representation and population should be high enough to reflect the diversity of interests within and among the states. Smith stated, moreover, that only the wealthiest and most socially prominent men would be elected to the House if the system of representation remained unaltered. Only the rich and their allies had the economic resources, personal reputation, and necessary family connections to compete for power within populous and extensive electoral districts.[29]

Anti-Federalist politicians of diverse views agreed that the proposed Congress was a threat to "equal liberty." As spokesmen and pamphleteers, they defined this concept in both negative and positive terms. They insisted that no group of citizens, particularly the wealthy, should derive special privileges through their political influence. The "Federal Farmer" declared his party's primary goals to be "equal liberty, and equal laws diffusing their influence among all orders of men."[30] The Anti-Federalists also defended the right of ordinary citizens, especially yeomen, to compete for power. "Cato" argued that the most effective barriers to aristocracy were "the equality of the laws . . . the frequency of elections, and the chance that everyone has in sharing in public business."[31] To Abraham Yates, Jr., the Declaration of Independence guaranteed equality to both individuals and to communities or states:

> We hold these truths to be self evident that all men are Created Equal. . . . The members of a civil community are Confederates, not subjects; and their Rulers Servants, not masters; and all Legitimate Government Consists in the dominion of equal laws made with common consent, that is in the dominion of men over themselves; not in the Dominion of Communities over Communities, or of any men over other men.[32]

The Anti-Federalists were practitioners of an eighteenth-century style of populism that was not fully democratic in a modern sense. They believed that only those citizens who owned some property were capable of participating responsibly in the political process. Smith, Clinton, and Yates themselves were men of middle-class origin who had gained political power and had achieved considerable wealth during the Revolution. Their own sense of social identity influenced their attitudes toward liberty as much as their individual economic interests did. Indeed, their political rhetoric often reflected the contradictions in their own experience as public figures. They all favored a system of government in which political preferment would not depend simply upon wealth and social influence. As their own example would suggest, however, the sons of farmers could challenge elite rule only after they had themselves become well-to-do.[33] At that point, their own personal rectitude or virtue alone could guarantee that they would be faithful servants of the people's liberties.

Most Anti-Federalist leaders in New York genuinely believed that their principal opponents favored an aristocratic form of politics. They expressed this theme in their private correspondence as well as in their pamphlets and speeches intended for the public. George Clinton described the debate in the Poughkeepsie convention as a conflict between "the friends of the rights of mankind" and the "the advocates of despotism." The governor's nephew and secretary, DeWitt Clinton, predicted that those people who presently supported the Constitution would pray for deliverance if the new system were adopted: "From the insolence of great men — from the tyranny of the rich — from the unfeeling rapacity of the excise-man and Tax-gatherer — from the misery of despotism — from the expense of supporting standing armies, navies, placemen, sinecures, federal cities, Senators, Presidents and a long train of et ceteras Good Lord deliver us!" Melancton Smith warned Abraham Yates not to expect the Anti-Federalists to prevail in the Massachusetts state convention even though their party probably had a majority of the delegates on its side: "I think it best always to reckon the strength of your adversaries as much as it is. The *better sort*, have means of *convincing* those who differ from them, with which I am unacquainted. And how prevalent these kinds of means may be, I cannot pretend to say. I confess I fear their power."[34]

Melancton Smith's defense of liberty is especially important because he led his party in debate during much of the Poughkeepsie convention. A farmer's son, he was an obscure merchant in Dutchess County on the eve of the Revolution. He commanded a Ranger corps against local Tories during the war and subsequently became a major figure in state politics. He also rose greatly in wealth, partly by employing sharp trading practices in selling supplies to the army. His case violates almost every economic criterion that Charles Beard used for identifying Anti-Federalists. By the mid-1780s, he was a wealthy merchant, a creditor, and a resident of New York City.[35] He identified politically, however, with middle-class citizens. In April, 1788, Smith appealed to the voters of New York to elect Anti-Federalist delegates to the state ratifying convention. Writing as "Plebian," he identified the opposition to the Constitution as the "cause of liberty and of mankind." He directed his message specifically to "you . . . the common people . . . the yeomanry of the country." He predicted that ordinary citizens would be the "principal losers, if the constitution should prove oppressive. . . . When a tyranny is established, there are always masters as well as slaves; the great and well-born are generally the former, and the middling class the latter."[36] Smith won election to the state convention by running as a candidate in Dutchess County rather than in New York City, a Federalist stronghold. The Anti-Federalists achieved their greatest electoral success among farmers in upstate counties by emphasizing the dangers of increased taxes and of an expanded bureaucracy under the proposed federal system.

Smith's first speech in the Poughkeepsie convention was characterized by both idealism and a sense of political realism. Stating that he valued "the liberties of his country" even above the Union, he denounced the Constitution for strengthening slavery and favoring aristocracy. To Smith, the three-fifths clause violated the basic principle of representation that only free persons could exercise a role in their own governance. It also rewarded "those people who were so wicked as to keep slaves" since the major slaveholding states would gain increased representation in Congress.[37] Despite these moralistic objections to slavery, Smith offered no amendment concerning the three-fifths clause, undoubtedly because he recognized that the issue of slavery could divide Anti-Federalists both within and outside of New York. He sought instead to remedy the aristocratic bias of Congress by altering the rule that there be no more than one representative for every 30,000 persons. He resolved that the ratio be fixed at one representative for every 20,000 persons until the House membership reached 300. Population would be determined according to the manner prescribed in Article 1, section 2, with the three-fifths clause. After the House membership exceeded three hundred, Congress would apportion representation among the states in proportion to the number of their inhabitants. Finally, Smith proposed that the first Congress include 130 rather than 65 representatives.[38]

Smith and other Anti-Federalist leaders were not opposed to the acquisition of wealth itself. They instead feared that the wealthy would destroy liberty by gaining control of a powerful central government that was not susceptible to popular influence. The Anti-Federalists' greatest contribution to the cause of popular rights was in challenging the concept of class rule in a republic. Melancton Smith's speech on this point in the New York state convention deserves to be quoted at length:

> But I may be asked, would you exclude the first class in the community [i.e., the wealthy] from any share in legislation? I answer, By no means. They

would be factious, discontented, and constantly disturbing the government. It would also be unjust. They have their liberties to protect, as well as others, and the largest share of property. But my idea is, that the Constitution should be so framed as to admit this class [into the House of Representatives], together with a sufficient number of the middling class to control them. You will then combine the abilities and honesty of the community, a proper degree of information, and a disposition to pursue the public good. A representative body, composed principally of respectable yeomanry, is the best possible security to liberty. When the interest of this part of the community is pursued, the public good is pursued, because the body of every nation consists of this class, and because the interest of both the rich and the poor are involved in that of the middling class. No burden can be laid on the poor but what will sensibly affect the middling class. Any law rendering property insecure would be injurious to them. When, therefore, this class in society pursue their own interest, they promote that of the public, for it is involved in it.[39]

Smith's argument rested on the belief that American society was based on class divisions despite the absence of a titled nobility. As he reminded his fellow delegates, "birth, education, talents, and wealth, create distinctions among men as visible, and of as much influence, as titles, stars, and garters." He labeled the privileged classes in America a "natural aristocracy" as opposed to the hereditary aristocracy in Europe. Favored by social background and wealth, the aristocracy developed a love of power and luxury that distinguished its way of life from the more frugal, moral habits of the middle classes. Smith argued that it would be dangerous to entrust government solely to the elite:

The latter do not feel for the poor and middling class; the reasons are obvious — they are not obliged to use the same pains and labor to procure property as the other. They feel not the inconveniences arising from the payment of small sums. The great consider themselves above the common people, entitled to more respect, do not associate with them; they fancy themselves to have a right of preeminence in every thing. In short, they possess the same feelings, and are under the influence of the same motives, as an hereditary nobility.[40]

Alexander Hamilton and Robert R. Livingston led the Federalist response to Smith. Although their arguments were sometimes brilliant rhetorically, they were inconsistent. Hamilton and Livingston denied that there was any aristocracy in American society. Had not the Revolution eliminated all legal distinctions and privileges based upon birth? Although stressing the equality of all citizens before the law, they also defended the social character of the upper classes and denigrated the poor. Hamilton expressed an eighteenth-century version of the trickle-down theory by maintaining that private vices could be public virtues. Although the wealthy man's taste for luxury might be considered morally suspect, his acquisitiveness helped to promote economic prosperity. The vices of the poor, by contrast, were often at the expense of public wealth.[41]

Robert R. Livingston expressed his class feeling even more forcefully than Hamilton:

> I am not interested in defending rich men: but what does he [i.e., Smith] mean by telling us that the rich are vicious and intemperate? Will he presume to point out to us the class of men in which intemperance is not to be found? Is there less intemperance in feeding on beef than on turtle? or in drinking rum than wine? I think the gentleman does not reason from facts. If he will look round among the rich men of his acquaintance, I fancy he will find them as honest and virtuous as any class in the community. He says the rich are unfeeling; I believe they are less so than the poor; for it seems to me probable that those who are most occupied by their own cares and distresses have the least sympathy with the distresses of others. The sympathy of the poor is generally selfish, that of the rich a more disinterested emotion.[42]

Both Hamilton and Livingston chose to ignore the heart of Smith's argument — that the middle classes should have a share in government. Few American politicians could afford publicly to deprecate the yeomen who constituted a major portion of the free population. Federalist leaders preferred instead to depict society as being divided between the virtuous and the vicious, the learned as opposed to the ignorant.

Robert R. Livingston mocked Smith's speech by posing a series of rhetorical questions: "Does a man possess the confidence of his fellow-citizens for having done them important services? He is an *aristocrat*. Has he great integrity? Such a man will be greatly trusted: he is an aristocrat. Indeed, to determine that one is an aristocrat, we will need only be assured he is a man of merit. But I hope we have many such. I hope, sir, we are all aristocrats." Livingston then went on to imply that Smith favored a type of government which would exclude the meritorious: "He [i.e., Smith] would have his government composed of other classes of men: where will we find them? Why, he must go out into the highways, and pick up the rogue and the robber; he must go to the hedges and ditches, and bring in the poor, the blind, and the lame."[43]

The debate between Melancton Smith and Robert R. Livingston was among the most emotionally charged exchanges during the New York state convention. The Anti-Federalist's verbal assault against aristocracy provoked an intemperate, visceral response from the manor lord. It is unthinkable that this type of exchange would have occurred among a gathering of leading politicians during the colonial era. Prior to the Revolution, the rules of the game were quite different. Gentlemen practiced the art of demagoguery against each other, but they refrained from castigating an entire social class as being unfit to represent the people.

Smith's speech reflected the fact that New York had experienced a democratic revolution. The war against Britain had forced the most conservative members of the elite into exile as Tories. An entirely new group of men, largely those of middle-class birth, aspired to political office on the state level. Melancton Smith himself was able to defend middle-class values because he had succeeded in rising above his social origins. He was a plainspoken, powerfully built man who refused to defer to the gentry despite his humble background and lack of formal education. He spoke for those who wished to prevent, in George Dangerfield's words, "a resurgence in state and national form of that privileged government that New York had experienced as a colony."[44]

Unlike the political situation in New York, some Anti-Federalists in other states attributed their defeat in 1788 to their opponents' superior political skills, social influence, and speaking abilities. Hugh Ledlie of Connecticut, for example, wrote of "Anti" delegates being browbeaten and awed by Federalist eloquence and political persuasion. How could men of the plow lacking a liberal education, he complained, overcome the power of the "self-interested gentry," these "great and mighty men"?[45] The political atmosphere was quite different in the New York state convention. Rather than being in awe of Federalist spokesmen, the leading Anti-Federalist delegates stood up to them in debate and ridiculed them in their private correspondence. George Clinton wrote to his friend, John Lamb, that he had time to pen a letter, while Alexander Hamilton, "the little Great Man [is] employed in repeating over parts of Publius [i.e., *The Federalist*] to us. . . ."[46]

The governor's nephew, DeWitt Clinton, took special delight in describing how Melancton Smith turned his wit against Chancellor Livingston. Smith's opportunity for ridicule came as he defended congressional power over the military but criticized the notion of congressional authority over taxation. The federal legislature, he declared, should not be given the power over both the sword and the purse. He then reminded the chancellor that there were "some people who had no great inclination to handle the sword, were notwithstanding very fond of thrusting their hands into the purse."[47] This remark was clearly aimed at Livingston, for he had not taken part in the fighting during the Revolution. The ferocity of Smith's oratory tended to obscure the limits of his radicalism. Although he sought to curtail Livingston's political influence, he had no intention of undermining the social system that was the basis of the landlord's economic power.

Federalists were not advocates of aristocracy in a European sense. They were comfortable with a deferential form of republican politics. Ordinary citizens could depend upon wealthy, educated men to defend their interests. As Hamilton argued in *The Federalist* (number 35):

> Mechanics and manufactures [i.e., artisans] will always be inclined, with few exceptions, to give their votes to merchants in preference to persons of their own professions or trades. . . . They know that the merchant is their natural patron or friend; and they are aware . . . that their interests can be more effectively promoted by the merchant than by themselves.[48]

This argument was not simply wishful thinking on Hamilton's part, but reflected certain political and social realities of the 1780s. New York City artisans helped to elect Federalist merchants to the state ratifying convention because they believed that the Constitution would promote economic prosperity.

The debate concerning representation in Congress was ironic in several ways. The Federalists proposed a popularly elected House of Representatives while favoring an elitist form of republicanism. The Anti-Federalists assumed the mantle of democracy even though they questioned the legitimacy of forming a representative assembly for the entire United States. Although they desired that farmers be elected to Congress, their proposed amendment offered no guarantee of this result. (Indeed, any such guarantee would have violated the Anti-

Federalist commitment to liberty.) One may question whether a substantial number of yeomen would have been elected to Congress even if the ratio between representation and population had been fixed at one per twenty thousand—the ratio that Melancton Smith first suggested in the New York ratifying convention. For reasons that the Anti-Federalists themselves recognized, the wealthy had an advantage in competing for national office that could not be erased simply by altering the method for determining representation in Congress.

Smith resembled other moderate Anti-Federalists in accepting the need for a bicameral legislature. The House would protect liberty by representing the citizens' needs and interests as closely as possible. The Senate would provide stability in government and, above all, would safeguard states' rights. Smith maintained that the state legislatures should be given the power of recalling senators. He also favored a constitutional amendment that senators be allowed to serve for no longer than six years in any period of twelve years. If senators were eligible for continual reappointment, only a small group of the most influential men would acquire experience in public affairs. The practice of rotation in office would ensure that senators remained dependent upon both the people and the state legislatures. It would also promote liberty by encouraging a broad range of citizens to hold high office. Smith believed that self-made men such as himself should compete for leadership with the well-born. He wished to broaden the membership of the Senate while retaining certain distinctions between the two houses of Congress. The House should include a substantial number of middle-class men, especially "respectable" yeomen. This feature would not be as necessary in the Senate. Smith's distinction between the House and Senate is similar to that offered by the "Federal Farmer." The latter described the House as the "democratic branch" dedicated to securing "personal liberty," the freedom of individual citizens from governmental oppression. The Senate instead would protect the interests of substantial property holders.[49]

Federalist spokesmen favored a representative system of government that would promote elite leadership. Robert R. Livingston objected to the practice of rotation in office for senators as an improper restriction upon freedom of political choice. If senators possessed the confidence of the people, why should they not be elected to a second or third consecutive term by state legislatures? To restrict the opportunity for reelection would, moreover, deprive senators of an important motive to promote the general welfare. Livingston characterized mandatory rotation as "an absurd species of ostracism — a mode of proscribing eminent merit, and banishing from stations of trust those who have filled them with the greatest faithfulness. . . . The acquisition of abilities is hardly worth the trouble, unless one is to enjoy the satisfaction of employing them for the good of one's country." In Livingston's view, the desire for personal honors and rewards was "the strongest stimulus to public virtue."[50]

Federalists believed there was a reciprocal relationship between the extent of national power and the character of national leadership. The central government needed to be sufficiently strong in order to attract the services of the most prominent and capable citizens. By wielding extensive powers, federal officials could then counteract the influence of incompetent or unscrupulous politicians in the state governments. Alexander Hamilton viewed the Anti-Federalist amendments concerning the Senate as a threat to both national unity and political stability. He regarded the recall of senators as an especially dangerous practice. National survival, he maintained, depended upon the "perpetual accommodation and sacrifice of local advantage to general expediency." A senator could never develop a nationalistic outlook if he was "a slave to all the capricious humors among the people." Hamilton argued that an overly democratic system of government was bound to be parochial and inconstant. Although the House of Representatives should be a democratic body, the Senate should be designed to "correct the prejudices, check the intemperate passions, and regulate the fluctuations, of a popular assembly."[51]

After the first national elections in late 1788, the Federalists gained control of Congress and the process of amending the Constitution. They easily defeated an Anti-Federalist proposal that the states control the election of senators on an annual basis.[52] There was to be no change in the institutions of government that would alter the federal system to the states' advantage. Congress was willing, however, to consider a constitutional amendment concerning apportionment in the House of Representatives. Federalists accepted some measure of democratic reform as long as this process did not elevate the states above the nation.

The federal legislature approved a preliminary version of the Bill of Rights in September, 1789. The proposed first amendment embodied the principle that the House of Representatives was both a democratic body and a select group of public servants. This complex amendment provided that membership in the House not fall below certain minimum levels as the population grew. There would be one representative for every thirty thousand persons until the House had one hundred members. (The three-fifths clause would be used in determining population.) The membership could never be reduced below two hundred once it reached that level. However, the amendment allowed Congress to alter the ratio between representation and population to prevent the House from becoming too unwieldy in numbers. Once the membership grew to two hundred members, there could be no more than one representative for every fifty thousand persons. By the end of 1791, eight states, including New York, had ratified this proposal. The amendment was nearly incorporated into the Constitution, but it failed to win the approval of three-fourths of the states.[53] The Anti-Federalist criticism of the new federal system almost led to a modest change in the method of apportioning representation in Congress. The demand to restrict congressional power, particularly in the area of taxation, elicited greater resistance.

THE POWER TO TAX

The issue of taxation was among the most important controversies between supporters and critics of the Constitution. Both Federalists and Anti-Federalists recognized that the authority of any government depended upon its power to tax. The Anti-Federalist author "Brutus" compared a government without the command of revenue to "an animal without blood, or the subsistence of one without food."[54] Alexander Hamilton put the matter even more bluntly in *The Federalist:* "A nation cannot long exist without revenue."[55] In attempting to establish a national taxing power, the Federalists sought a fundamental change in the balance of power between the central government and the states. Under the Articles of Confederation, Congress lacked the authority to tax and therefore depended upon the states to provide funds for the common treasury. By the mid-1780s, the system of raising revenue through requisitions had clearly failed. The Constitution marked a radical departure from the Confederation by authorizing Congress "To lay and collect Taxes, Duties, Imposts and Excises, to pay the Debts and Provide for the common Defence and general Welfare of the United States." Moreover, the states were prohibited from imposing customs duties upon either imports or exports without the consent of Congress except for the purpose of executing inspection laws. Congress obtained exclusive jurisdiction, but not unlimited power over external taxation — the raising of revenue from trade with foreign countries. Article 1, section 9, prohibited the national legislature from collecting any taxes upon goods exported from any state. The congressional power to tax foreign trade applied to imports alone.[56]

The Constitution implicitly recognized that Congress and the state governments would share jurisdiction over two principal types of internal taxation: excises and direct taxes. Eighteenth-century politicians understood the excise to mean a tax upon certain goods that were produced for popular consumption, such as alcoholic beverages. This type of tax was indirect because producers passed on its cost to consumers by charging higher prices on retail goods. In the case of the direct tax, the government's power over the individual citizen was immediate. This form of taxation ordinarily required the individual to pay the tax collector directly for either the ownership of property or for the number of persons living within one's household.[57] The Constitution vested Congress with the general power of taxation, but it stipulated that neither a poll tax nor any other type of direct tax be levied except in proportion to the census taken once every ten years. Each state's share of taxation was to be determined according to its entire free population and three-fifths of all slaves. This complex method of apportioning taxation was neither wholly nationalistic nor federal in design. The Congress might tax individual citizens directly, but it could do so only by considering them as residents of a particular state.

Nearly all Anti-Federalists believed that the Constitution allowed Congress far too much authority to tax. They also agreed about the evils implicit in this system — the weakening of state power, the enrichment of federal officials at the common people's expense, and the decline of public morality. Although Anti-Federalist leaders in New York shared a common ideological perspective, their commitment to liberty barely masked the differences within their party. They dreaded the prospect of a supreme national government, but they held conflicting ideas about the need to enhance federal power.

George Clinton's support of Congress was often conditional during the mid- to late 1780s. In 1786, he was willing to support a congressional impost or import duty, provided that state officials had the responsibility for collecting it. He approached the ratification of the Constitution in the same spirit; he was prepared to approve the Constitution, provided that his state's ratification be conditional upon limiting federal power, including the authority to tax. His belief in state government as the guardian of liberty bolstered his efforts to maintain New York's economic and political independence.

Abraham Yates's opposition to a federal taxing power was more absolute than Clinton's. Writing as "Sidney" in 1785, he warned that even a limited congressional impost would signal *"the death warrant of American liberty!"*[58] His rejection of the Constitution was both predictable and consistent with his earlier beliefs.

Although Melancton Smith had opposed the federal impost in the mid-1780s, he modified his views toward congressional taxation during the debate concerning the Constitution. Unlike Yates, he accepted the political and financial necessity of granting some degree of taxing power to Congress. He actively supported a constitutional amendment that would restrict rather than prohibit this power. His zeal for liberty was tempered by his loyalty to the Union.

It would be a mistake to underestimate the change in New York politics that resulted from the British withdrawal at the war's end. Some politicians who had previously demanded that federal power be increased now came to identify themselves as the staunchest defenders of states' rights. In March, 1781, New York had been among the first states to approve a federal request authorizing Congress to levy an import duty of 5 percent on foreign goods. Governor Clinton speedily transmitted the state legislature's action to Congress. Few patriots could tolerate a weak central government as long as the enemy remained in control of nearly the entire southern district, including Manhattan. The urgency of supporting Congress weakened as the war came to an end. In April, 1783, the state legislature repealed its approval of the impost.

After the British evacuation in November, the state soon began to obtain a major share of its revenues from its own customs duties. With income from tariffs and land sales, New York accumulated a surplus in its treasury, kept taxes to a minimum, and assumed a major portion of the national debt owned by its citizens. It is therefore not surprising that Governor Clinton and his supporters resisted the enactment of a federal impost between 1783 and 1787. They undoubtedly feared that their state might find it difficult to tax trade if Congress competed for this source of income. When the state legislature finally approved the impost in 1786, it insisted that the customs collectors be appointed by and be responsible to the state alone. Congress refused to accept this condition, but failed to convince New York to change its position.[59] The opposition of New York alone defeated the impost in 1786 and 1787, just as Rhode Island had blocked a similar measure five years earlier. If the federal government had received the authority to tax imports, it is doubtful that so many politicians would have favored a more extensive plan to increase national power. The Clintonians' refusal to cooperate with Congress was a shortsighted policy that was to have disastrous consequences for the cause of states' rights.

Clinton himself believed that state sovereignty was not inconsistent with an efficient, well-financed federal government. The governor was proud of his state's financial support of the Union. New York paid a higher proportion of its requisitions to Congress than any other state did during the period 1785–88.[60] Clinton pronounced himself ready to support a congressional impost if the states controlled the purse strings through the appointment of customs collectors. His position was not designed simply to prevent passage of the import duty while blaming Congress for political deadlock. He wished to strengthen the Confederation without weakening his state's liberty or independence. By the summer of 1788, that goal was no longer possible.

During the New York state ratifying convention, the Federalists attempted to embarrass Clinton by contrasting his current opposition to the Constitution with his former support of Congress during the Revolutionary War. Alexander Hamilton requested that the secretary of the convention read a series of state papers, including two messages from the governor to the legislature that expressed the need to strengthen the Confederation between 1780 and 1782.[61] Clinton explained this apparent inconsistency by emphasizing the differences in circumstances between the war years and the present situation:

> Because a strong government was wanted during the late war, does it follow that we should now be obliged to accept of a dangerous one? I ever

lamented the feebleness of the Confederation, for this reason, among others, that the experience of its weakness would one day drive the people into an adoption of a constitution dangerous to our liberties. . . . If the gentleman can show me that the proposed Constitution is a safe one, I will drop all opposition.[62]

Although the governor left no surviving record of his political strategy, he seems to have entered the state ratifying convention with three main goals: preventing the ratification of the Constitution in its original form, approving the new federal system if it could be sufficiently modified by amendment, and avoiding political responsibility if the convention should result in stalemate. The need to maintain party unity helps to explain why he neglected certain issues while stressing others. He declined to criticize the proposed federal system for depriving the states of certain key powers, particularly the authority to enact customs duties or to issue paper money. His silence on these issues should not be interpreted as approval of these constitutional restrictions. If he had raised these points, he might have provoked a divisive debate among his fellow Anti-Federalists about the precise balance between federal power and states' rights. He emphasized instead the dangers that a powerful national government would pose in general to state sovereignty and individual liberty. He urged his state to adopt the new governmental system on condition that certain important federal powers be restricted until a new constitutional convention was held. After stating his opposition to the Constitution, he declared his support for this proposal "from a strong attachment to the Union — from a spirit of conciliation and an earnest desire to promote peace and harmony."[63] During the remainder of the convention, he remained committed to a policy of compromise that the opposition party could not possibly accept. He finally was less interested in reforming the Constitution than in preventing the establishment of a supreme national government. He therefore had ample reason to reject Melancton Smith's motion of July 26 to endorse the Constitution with a series of recommendations for change.

Unlike George Clinton, Abraham Yates never modified his stance toward federal taxation. He voted against the congressional impost in the state legislature even during the war. When the call for the impost was revived in 1783, he expressed little faith in his opponents' claims that Congress sought a modest grant of authority. It mattered little to him that the central government requested only the right to impose customs duties over a period of twenty-five years in order to pay off the United States debt contracted during the war. His own understanding of history convinced him that federal officials eventually would use the impost as a means of gaining the power to tax on a permanent and general basis. As Congress accumulated additional debts, it would again demand that the level of taxation be increased. This process would lead to the loss of individual freedom as well as to the insolvency of state government. Because the burden of federal taxation would fall most heavily on the middle classes, the gap between the rich and poor would be magnified. The American experiment in republican government could endure only if the free population retained its economic independence. Once the people were deprived of their property, they could no longer resist their rulers' lust for power. They would themselves become corrupted by a desire to advance their material well-being at the price of liberty.[64]

Abraham Yates's commitment to liberty was based upon an intensely personal view of politics. Born in Albany in 1724, he was the son of an ordinary burgher. He knew from his own experience of the power that the "great" wielded over the "small." His early career owed much to the support of Robert Livingston, Jr., the lord of Livingston Manor. As a sheriff in the 1750s, Yates had evicted squatters from his patron's land and upheld New York law against Yankee intruders from New England. He never accepted, however, the notion that he was anyone's servant. By the early 1760s, he was already writing a manuscript that blamed the manor system for many of the colony's problems.[65] As he rose in wealth and prominence, he retained his loyalty to the common people. He also provoked his political opponents to outrage with his appeals to popular support against aristocracy. In 1777, General Philip Schuyler commented with disdain to Alexander Hamilton that Yates, a former shoemaker's apprentice ("the late Cobler [sic] of Laws and Old Shoes"), held many appointive offices in Albany County and was to be nominated for lieutenant governor.[66] Writing to Robert Morris in 1782, Hamilton characterized Yates as "a man whose ignorance and perverseness are only surpassed by his pertinacity and conceit." Hamilton attributed Yates's electoral success to demogoguery: "The people have been a long time in the *habit* of choosing him in different offices; and to the title of prescription, he adds that of being a preacher to their taste. He *assures* them, they are too poor to pay taxes."[67]

It should be noted that Yates's personal behavior was generally consistent with his political ideals. For example, he became a severe critic of Robert Morris's administration after failing to obtain an appointment as Receiver of Continental Taxes. Since he saw himself as being punished for his states' rights views, he associated his own liberty with the struggle against congressional power. He opposed nearly all nationalistic measures when he later represented his state in Congress.[68]

By the mid-1780s, Yates had come to view any attempt to increase congressional power as a conspiracy against liberty. The advocates of a federal taxing power, he wrote in 1785 and 1786, intended no less than to undermine the Revolution by instituting the British system of government in America. Yates was not so literal-minded as to believe that Morris and his allies sought to establish a precise replica of the British Constitution. He maintained instead that the proposal to fund the United States debt through a series of tariffs was based upon monarchical principles. He identified the difference between the British and American forms of government as moral in nature. A monarchy promoted "extravagance and luxury" through methods founded upon "duplicity and partiality." A republic instead encouraged "frugality and economy" since its fundamental principles were "virtue and equality."[69] Morris's funding scheme smacked of monarchy because it used the same methods that the English crown employed to expand its power after the Glorious Revolution of 1688. The executive first succeeded in convincing Parliament to raise taxes to meet interest payments on the national debt. The royal administration then used these revenues as means of extending its political influence over the legislature. The increase of government expenditures served the self-interest of pensioners and placemen (bureaucrats), but it imposed an economic burden on the tax-paying classes, particularly the common people.

Yates believed that monarchical government was inherently corrupt because it enticed rulers to advance their power at the people's expense. Although a republic was not characterized by equality in property-holding, it was marked by an identity of interests between all classes of citizens. Citizens would devote themselves to the public good only if they could not procure special privileges by simply doing the government's bidding.[70]

Yates's use of the pseudonyms "Sidney" and "Rough Hewer" succinctly expressed his political philosophy. Algernon Sidney (1622–83) was among the most eloquent defenders of constitutional government in late seventeenth-century England. Both his life and his writings served as an example to many American Whigs during the revolutionary era. Executed for his alleged role in plotting to overthrow Charles II, he was best remembered for defending the people's right to resist tyrants. One historian, Caroline Robbins, has characterized his posthumously published *Discourses on Government* as a "textbook of revolution." Yates himself admired a statement attributed to Sidney: "While I live I shall endeavor to preserve my liberty. . . . I hope I shall dye [*sic*] in the same principle in which I have lived."[71]

The pseudonym "Rough Hewer" seems to have had both positive and negative connotations. Yates regarded himself as a proud, independent man — a "rough hewer"— who was unafraid to use his pen as a weapon in defense of liberty. He also identified with the common people — those who might be reduced by an oppressive government to the condition of "hewers of wood and drawers of water." His vision of an unjust society was one in which rulers rode roughshod over the masses. If Congress gained the power to tax, he wrote in 1785, the people would soon be employed in building roads for rich men's coaches. They would themselves be too poor to afford any livestock but pigs.[72]

Yates was a self-educated man who regarded historical proof as an essential element in political analysis. He quoted extensively from both ancient and modern sources to prove his basic thesis — that tyrants inevitably seek to strengthen rule by gaining absolute control over the raising of revenue. Because Yates believed that a single pattern of events controlled all history, he saw nothing incongruous in referring to the pharaoh of Egypt in one sentence and Philip II of Spain in the next. He was convinced that America was liable to suffer from the same greed and corruption that had plagued other lands. Americans would be mistaken if they believed that they were intrinsically more virtuous than Europeans; they were simply more fortunate than their Old World counterparts because their society was more egalitarian. The United States' survival as a republic depended upon yeomen and artisans — middle-class citizens who possessed sufficient property to be indepen-

dent but who had not become corrupted by riches.[73] Other Anti-
Federalists agreed with Yates. "Centinel" wrote that a "republican,
or free government, can only exist where the body of the people are
virtuous, and where property is pretty equally divided."[74]

Yates believed that the middle classes would be secure in their property and liberty only if the United States adopted his definition of federalism. It would be dangerous to give the same group of rulers that
power over both the purse and the sword. Because Congress already
had the power under the Articles of Confederation to declare war and
to raise troops, it should not also be given the power to tax. While the
federal government weakened in 1786, Yates was imagining schemes
to restrict congressional power still further. Fearing that the national
debt might become permanent, he proposed that Congress be prohibited from borrowing money or issuing bills of credit unless it first obtained the consent of all thirteen state legislatures.[75]

Considering Yates's extreme opposition to the federal impost, he
was bound to be a severe critic of the Constitution. Throughout the
debate over ratification, he remained true to his principles by adopt-
ing a negative attitude to the proposed change in government. Because he had previously denounced the federal impost as a tyrannical
measure, he could hardly accept a Constitution that granted Congress
the unlimited authority to enact customs duties and other taxes. After
the Constitution was ratified, he retired from national politics rather
than taint himself by contact with a "corrupt" system. During his
term as mayor of Albany before his death in 1796, he devoted much
of his time to the writing of history, including an account of the period from 1778 to 1793. Analyzing the adoption of the Constitution
in conspiratorial terms, he viewed the Hamiltonian system of finance
as the finishing blow to liberty.[76] His greatest error was to attribute
malicious motives to the men who drafted the new Constitution. He
could not admit that the advocates of national power were influenced
by a desire to protect American freedom.

Unlike Abraham Yates, Melancton Smith recognized in 1788 the
importance of compromising with the proponents of nationalism. In
a pamphlet written for the general public in April, he admitted that
the Articles of Confederation were inadequate to the preservation of
the Union. He also stated that the United States would be unable to
drive the British from the northwest forts until the central government

possessed sufficient strength and resources. Having conceded the need for reform, he maintained that the country was not in such dire straits that the Constitution should be ratified in its original form. He predicted that granting Congress the power to regulate trade and to levy customs duties would not bring prosperity. The citizens of New York should not look to government for solutions to their economic problems; they should instead strengthen their commitment to "frugality and industry." Smith also warned that the tax burden on the middle classes would become oppressive if Congress was given the unlimited power to raise revenue. If the Constitution was adopted without amendments, citizens should be prepared for the "continental tax-gatherer knocking at their doors."[77]

Although Smith stirred popular fears of congressional taxation during an election campaign, he also prepared to work for reform of the Constitution. During the fall of 1787, the moderate Anti-Federalist position concerning taxation was outlined in "Federal Farmer" letters and "Brutus" essays.[78] Both series of newspaper articles, as noted above, bear a striking similarity to the rhetoric that Melancton Smith subsequently used in criticizing the Constitution during the New York state convention. Whoever it was who used these pseudonyms, both the "Federal Farmer" and "Brutus" argued that the Constitution should distinguish between the levying of external and internal taxes. Congress might be granted sole authority over customs duties provided that its taxing power was largely confined to this area. "Brutus" maintained that federal tariffs posed little danger to liberty because they could be collected in a few seaports by a small number of officials. The impost would not lead to a major increase in the size of government bureaucracy. "Brutus" also noted that market forces would tend to keep the level of these duties within reasonable bounds. If Congress attempted to raise the impost too much, government revenues would fall because merchants would either reduce their foreign orders or else they would resort to smuggling.

The problems presented by federal control over internal taxation were far greater than from those concerning import duties. The former type of taxes, Brutus explained, included "poll taxes, land taxes, excises, duties on written instruments, on every thing we eat, drink, or wear; they take hold of every species of property, and come home to every man's house and pocket. These are often so oppressive, as to grind the face of the poor, and render the lives of the common people a burden to them."[79] "Brutus" argued that the federal government should not exercise any power over internal taxation. The "Federal Farmer" conceded this power to the Union only if the states failed to comply with federal requisitions — monies raised by the states to meet national needs in special circumstances. Congress could not be trusted to determine a just policy of internal taxation because it would be dominated by a small group of wealthy men. State governments alone fairly represented the people's interests. "Brutus" linked state sovereignty to the protection of ordinary citizens' rights. The security of liberty required that spheres of governmental responsibility be kept distinct. Congress would apply customs revenues toward payment of the United States debt, support of the general government, and the defense of the Union. State governments would control all other forms of taxation for their own domestic needs and concerns.[80]

In the New York state ratifying convention, Melancton Smith argued that the state governments would eventually collapse if Congress were given an unlimited power of taxation. He urged repeatedly that the states be given exclusive control over some specific sources of revenue.[81] Alexander Hamilton countered that the national government could not execute its responsibilities if it were prohibited from taxing certain resources. He strongly objected to the Anti-Federalist proposal of relying upon requisitions in national emergencies. This system had nearly led to the destruction of the country during the war and the Confederation era. The federal government must not be dependent upon the states for revenue. "All confidence and credit" in Congress would be destroyed by "obliging the government to ask, instead of empowering them to command." If the power to tax was limited, the government would instead need to borrow. This practice again could result only in national weakness. State governments lacked the need for taxing powers as broad as the federal government's since their responsibilities were less "numerous, extensive, and important":

> Have they to provide against foreign invasion? Have they to maintain fleets and armies? Have they any concern in the regulation of commerce, the procuring alliances, or forming treaties of peace? No. Their objects are merely civil and domestic — to support the legislative establishment, and to provide for the administration of the laws.[82]

The exchange between Smith and Hamilton represented a subtle inversion of the debate between Whig and Tory spokesmen over parliamentary taxation during the pre-Revolutionary era. Between 1765 and 1774, Americans insisted that their liberty would be secure only if there were a clear demarcation between parliamentary power and the jurisdiction of their own colonial assemblies. Although they accepted Parliament's right to impose customs duties for the regulation of trade, they demanded that their own legislatures exercise sole control over taxation. In 1788, Melancton Smith conceded more authority to the federal government than many Americans had been willing to allow Parliament twenty years previously. Smith acknowledged the right of Congress to levy customs duties for revenue as long as the central government did not interfere with the internal taxation of the states. He nevertheless maintained the notion that the sovereign powers of the general and local governments should remain distinct: "I have no more conception, that in taxation, two powers can act together, than that two bodies can occupy the same place."[83]

Hamilton advocated an entirely new federal system by insisting that the central government and the states could share jurisdiction over internal taxation. He meanwhile continued to favor the traditional British notion that the central authority alone should regulate the external commerce of the empire. Because Americans now had control of their own federal government, they could trust it to tax as well as to exercise fairly other powers over foreign trade.

Melancton Smith was among a group of moderate Anti-Federalists who accepted a limited expansion of federal authority as the price of securing the independence of the states. The stakes of power had shifted between 1767 and 1787. The question before the American people was no longer one involving the claims of a distant Parliament. The issue was instead the extent to which Congress would gain additional taxing powers along with control over external commerce.

Anti-Federalist delegates to the Poughkeepsie convention did not rule out a federal excise or direct federal taxation altogether. They acknowledged the central government's financial needs while seeking to protect state sovereignty. The convention approved a constitutional amendment to prohibit the excise on all domestic manufactures except ardent spirits — the most likely products to be taxed by Congress. New York also adopted the same proposal that three state conventions had previously passed. This amendment would prohibit direct federal taxation unless revenues from customs duties or excises were insufficient for national purposes. Congress was not to levy direct taxes before it had attempted to raise the necessary sums through requisitions on the states. Federalist delegates voted for their opponents' recommendations as their only means of securing the ratification of the Constitution.[84]

Because Federalists dominated the first Congress elected under the Constitution, the new government's critics had little prospect of achieving their most radical demands. Both the House and Senate rejected an Anti-Federalist proposal to restrict direct federal taxation as the New York state convention had desired.[85] Although Federalists conceded the need to protect individual liberties in the Bill of Rights, they refused to budge on the issue of federal taxation.

The rapid demise of Anti-Federalism in 1789 has led some historians to minimize the political differences between the critics of the Constitution and their opponents. According to this argument, the contending parties during the ratification controversy merely favored distinct means of promoting the same general goal — the preservation of liberty within the Union. This view is correct in that nearly all American politicians shared a general commitment to such principles as federalism, representative government, and the rule of law. One should not, however, mistake the ratification of the Constitution — even with the addition of the Bill of Rights — as a genuine compromise between two competing groups.

The Anti-Federalists failed to secure passage of constitutional amendments for the purpose of restricting the federal government's enumerated powers. The structure of the new federal system remained unaltered. Critics of the Constitution simply had to accept the demise of the Confederation if they were to exercise any degree of influence in national politics after 1789. Only the most zealous libertarians — such as Abraham Yates — refused to make peace with the new order. The majority of Anti-Federalists soon recognized that they had ample opportunity to advance their own version of states' rights under the Constitution. George Clinton teamed up with his one-time opponent, Robert R. Livingston, in opposing the federal assumption of state debts in 1790. The former Anti-Federalist leader emerged as a stalwart of the Republican party during the early 1790s; he eventually died in 1812 while holding the office of vice-president of the United States.[86]

The history of American politics between 1789 and 1861, particularly after 1800, proved that the Anti-Federalists exaggerated the threat of national power. Consider the issue of taxation. During the early national period, the federal government received the greatest portion of its revenues from the tariff and the sale of western lands. When Congress imposed an excise on whiskey in 1791, it encountered resistance among western farmers. Although the government suppressed the Whiskey Rebellion in Pennsylvania in 1794, it soon recognized the limits of its authority. After the Republicans gained power in 1801, Congress repealed the whiskey tax and all other internal federal taxes. Most American politicians in the period before the Civil War accepted the notion that the federal legislature could tax domestic products and trade only during periods of national emergency.[87] The national government also had to retreat after it sought to restrict free speech and the free press. The Alien and Sedition Acts of 1798 proved a largely ineffective, counterproductive, and short-lived means of curbing internal dissent. The Jeffersonian persecution of Federalists in the early 1800s was equally misguided and inept.[88] In a general sense, the national government continually was at the mercy of rival state interests in the period before the Civil war. Hamilton was therefore quite farsighted when he argued in 1788 that the states still possessed sufficient power under the Constitution to threaten the dissolution of the Union.[89]

Anti-Federalist leaders commonly expressed a belief that the political framework established at the birth of a nation would determine the fate of generations. They therefore counseled extreme caution in granting power to the proposed national government. Critics of the Constitution found little comfort in the fact that George Washington would almost assuredly be the first president under the new government. As the essayist "Brutus" noted, "constitutions are not so necessary to regulate the conduct of good rulers as to restrain that of bad ones."[90] A Connecticut Anti-Federalist explained that "all might be well" if Washington was elected, "but perhaps after him Genl. Slushington might be the next or second president."[91] Abraham Yates opposed the granting of an impost to Congress in 1786 for similar reasons. Although the present government might not abuse its power, its actions would not guarantee the survival of liberty. Yates warned that a future Congress, one "less virtuous than the present," might "extend their civil list, encrease [sic] the salaries of their officers, multiply pensioners and placemen, keep up even in times of peace . . . useless fleets and armies, [and] engage in unnecessary and ruinous wars."[92]

Some Anti-Federalist authors advised that the Constitution be scrutinized carefully because the American people would be less able to resist governmental power in the future. "Cato" reminded his readers that the "progress of a commercial society begets luxury, the parent of inequality, the foe to virtue, and the enemy to restraint."[93] The Anti-Federalists' knowledge of history taught them that the people would not recover their liberties in the future if they relinquished them in the present.

The Anti-Federalists were, of course, hardly alone among American politicians in declaring their concern for future generations. The men who drafted the Constitution announced their intent of forming "a more perfect union" in order to "secure the Blessings of Liberty to ourselves and our Posterity." The founding fathers believed that the United States could best protect its freedom by creating a national government. Alexander Hamilton, one of the most extreme nationalists, maintained that the political struggle over the Constitution concerned "the fate of an empire," and not solely the existence of the Union. He argued that the states had to yield certain powers to the national government if the United States was to compete successfully in a world dominated by rival nations. The future of American economic growth depended upon the government's capacity to assert its military strength in international politics.[94]

The Anti-Federalists approached the problem of national power from a different perspective than did Hamilton. Although they also believed that the Union was essential to the maintenance of American independence, they feared that the growth of empire could lead to the loss of liberty. "Brutus" warned that the pursuit of military glory could result in the needless destruction of life, the impoverishment of the people through oppressive taxation, and the rise of permanent, professional armies in peacetime. Although he justified the concept of defensive war, he advised that the American people could best serve their interests by remaining true to their ideals: "We ought to furnish the world with the example of a great people, who in their civil institutions hold chiefly in view, the attainment of virtue, and happiness among ourselves."[95] Patrick Henry expressed a similar idea in the Virginia ratifying convention by contrasting the goals of liberty and empire:

> If we admit this Consolidated Government [i.e., the Constitution] it will be because we like a great [and] splendid one. Some way or other we must be a great and mighty empire; we must have an army, and a navy, and a number of things; When the American spirit was in its youth, the language of America was different: Liberty, Sir, was then the primary object.[96]

The Anti-Federalists believed that the federal government could best contribute to American liberty by keeping the demands on citizens to a minimum — by knowing when to leave the people alone. Patrick Henry, Melancton Smith, and their allies commonly referred to the following biblical passage as representing their social ideal: "But they shall sit every man under his vine and under his fig tree, and none shall make them afraid."[97] In the course of American history, that vision has become ever more a dream than a reality.

NOTES

1. The most thorough compendium of Anti-Federalist writings and speeches is Herbert J. Storing, ed., *The Complete Anti-Federalist*, 7 vols. (Chicago: University of Chicago Press, 1981). (The first volume, *What the Anti-Federalists Were For*, is the editor's introduction to the series.) For several important secondary works on Anti-Federalism, see James H. Hutson, "Country, Court, and Constitution: Antifederalism and the Historians," *William and Mary Quarterly (WMQ)*, 3rd ser., 38 (July, 1981): 337–68; Cecelia M. Kenyon, "Men of Little Faith: The Anti-Federalists on the Nature of Representative Government," *WMQ*, 3rd ser., 12 (January, 1955): 3–43; "The Political Thought of the Antifederalists," in *The Antifederalists*, ed. Cecelia M. Kenyon (Indianapolis: Bobbs-Merrill, 1966), xxi–cxvi; Jackson Turner Main, *The Antifederalists: Critics of the Constitution, 1781–1788* (Chapel Hill: University of North Carolina Press, 1961); Robert Allen Rutland, *The Ordeal of the Constitution: The Antifederalists and the Ratification Struggle of 1787–1788* (Norman: University of Oklahoma Press, 1966); Gordon S. Wood, *The Creation of the American Republic, 1776–1787* (Chapel Hill: University of North Carolina Press, 1969), pt. 5.

2. Lee to John Lamb, June 27, 1788, John Lamb Papers, New-York Historical Society (NYHS).

3. Michael Kammen, *Spheres of Liberty: Changing Perceptions of Liberty in American Culture* (Madison: University of Wisconsin Press, 1986), pt. 1; see also Forrest McDonald, *Novus Ordo Seclorum: The Intellectual Origins of the Constitution* (Lawrence: University Press of Kansas, 1985), 36–39.

4. Storing, *Complete Anti-Federalist*, 2:261.

5. See Jonathan Elliot, ed., *The Debates in the Several State Conventions on the Adoption of the Federal Constitution . . .* , 5 vols. (1836; Philadelphia: Lippincott, 1937), 2:297, 301.

6. Clinton Rossiter, ed., *The Federalist Papers* (New York: New American Library, 1961), no. 1, 35.

7. Kenyon, "Men of Little Faith"; McDonald, "The Anti-Federalists, 1781–1789," *Wisconsin Magazine of History*, 46 (Spring, 1963): 206–14. McDonald's recent work on the intellectual origins of the Constitution only briefly touches upon Anti-Federalism (*Novus Ordo Seclorum*, 284–85).

8. Wood, *Creation of the American Republic*, 516, and "Interests and Disinterestedness in the Making of the Constitution," in *Beyond Confederation: Origins of the Constitution and American National Identity*, ed. Richard Beeman, Stephen Botein, and Edward C. Carter II (Chapel Hill: University of North Carolina Press, 1987), 70.

9. For an analysis of this scholarship, see Hutson, "Country, Court, and Constitution," 338–45.

10. Edward Countryman, *A People in Revolution: The American Revolution and Political Society in New York, 1760–1790* (Baltimore: Johns Hopkins University Press, 1981), 134.

11. Alfred F. Young, *The Democratic-Republicans of New York: The Origins, 1763–1797* (Chapel Hill: University of North Carolina Press, 1967), 34–39.

12. Storing, *Complete Anti-Federalist*, 2:230; Wood, "Interests and Disinterestedness," 102.

13. Storing, *Complete Anti-Federalist*, 2:253.

14. The most recent general account of the ratification struggle in New York can be found in Stephen L. Schechter, ed., *The Reluctant Pillar: New York and the Adoption of the Federal Constitution* (Troy, N.Y.: Russell Sage College, 1985). See, in particular, the essays by John P. Kaminski, "New York: The Reluctant Pillar," 48–117, and by Gaspare J. Saladino, "A Guide to Sources for Studying the Ratification of the Constitution by New York State," 118–47. In addition to the scholarly works on New York history previously cited, see Stephen Boyd, *The Politics of Opposition and the Acceptance of the Constitution* (Millwood, N.Y.: KTO Press, 1979), chap. 3–4, 6; Robin Brooks, "Alexander Hamilton, Melancton Smith, and the Ratification of the Constitution in New York," *WMQ*, 3rd ser., 24 (July, 1967): 339–58; Linda Grant DePauw, *The Eleventh Pillar: New York State and the Federal Constitution* (Ithaca, N.Y.: Cornell University Press, 1966). See also DePauw's essays: "The Anticlimax of Antifederalism: The Abortive Second Convention Movement, 1788–89," *Prologue*, 2 (1970): 98–114, and "E. Wilder Spaulding and New York History," *New York History*, 49 (April, 1968): 142–55; Staughton Lynd, *Anti-Federalism in Dutchess County, New York* (Chicago: Loyola University Press, 1962); Richard B. Morris, "John Jay and the Adoption of the Federal Constitution in New York: A New Reading of Persons and Events," *New York History*, 63 (April, 1982): 133–64; E. Wilder Spaulding, *New York in the Critical Period, 1783–1789* (New York: Columbia University Press, 1932).

15. *Debates*, 1:319–37; 3:652–61. The Anti-Federalists of Pennsylvania and Maryland also drafted lists of amendments, but these proposals failed to win approval by their state conventions. See Edward Dumbauld, *The Bill of Rights and What It Means Today* (Norman: University of Oklahoma Press, 1957), 10–33, Appendix 4.

16. Kenyon, "Political Thought of the Antifederalists," lxxvi–lxxxvi; Storing, *Complete Anti-Federalist*, 1:48–61.

17. *Debates*, 1:319–37; 3:652–61. Rhode Island subsequently joined New York in proposing the recall of senators. North Carolina and Rhode Island adopted amendments to restrict federal taxation when they ratified the Constitution. See Dumbauld, *Bill of Rights*, 31–32.

18. Nelson, "Reason and Compromise in the Establishment of the Federal Constitution, 1787–1801," *WMQ*, 3rd ser., 44 (July, 1987): 476–79. Linda Grant DePauw had previously advanced a similar argument for New York. See *Eleventh Pillar*, xiii, 176–78.

19. For the "Brutus" essays, see Storing, *Complete Anti-Federalist*, 2:358–452. Although Paul Leicester Ford long ago suggested that Robert Yates was "Brutus," William Jeffrey, Jr., more recently has argued that Melancton Smith was the probable author. See Jeffrey, "The Letters of 'Brutus'– a Neglected Element in the Ratification Campaign of 1787–88," *University of Cincinnati Law Review*, 40 (1971): 643–46. I favor Jeffrey's interpretation on the basis of consistency in style and argument between the "Brutus" essays and Smith's speeches. Robert H. Webking has proposed that Smith was the "Federal Farmer" but not necessarily "Brutus" ("Melancton Smith and the *Letters from the Federal Farmer*," *WMQ*, 3rd ser., 44 [July, 1987]: 510–28). Webking indicates that Smith and the "Federal Farmer" analyzed the issue of representation in similar terms. I am, however, not convinced that Smith wrote the "Federal Farmer" essays. The prose style of the "Farmer" is more ornate and more replete with classical allusions than is Smith's. The more plainspoken Smith quoted from the Bible, a practice fairly common in "Brutus" but not in the "Federal Farmer." Smith and "Brutus" denounced slavery in similar terms, but the "Federal Farmer" avoided this subject. The "Federal Farmer" may not have been Richard Henry Lee (the customarily cited author), but he was not necessarily Smith. See also Wood, "The Authorship of *The Letters from the Federal Farmer*," *WMQ*, 3rd ser., 31 (April, 1974): 299–308.

20. Abraham Yates to Abraham G. Lansing, May 28, 1788, Abraham Yates Papers, New York Public Library (NYPL).

21. Storing, *Complete Anti-Federalist*, 6:89–121. "Sidney" was also sometimes spelled "Sydney."

22. Ibid., 2:101–29; Historians have usually ascribed the "Cato" essays to George Clinton. See, for example, Spaulding, *New York in the Critical Period*, 107–108. Linda Grant DePauw argues that Abraham Yates rather than Clinton wrote these essays (DePauw, *Eleventh Pillar*, Appendix A). The "Cato" essays express political attitudes that can be attributed to either Clinton or Yates. For example, Clinton criticized aristocracy in 1789 in terms almost identical to those used by "Cato" in 1787. Compare the passage in "Cato" (Storing, *Complete Anti-Federalist*, 2:122) to Clinton's remarks to Rufus King (Young, *Democratic-Republicans*, 4).

23. Storing, *Complete Anti-Federalist*, 2:382.

24. *Debates*, June 21, 1788, 2:262.

25. Storing, *Complete Anti-Federalist*, 2:111–12.

26. "Letters and Speeches, 1787–1788, relating to the New York State Constitutional Convention," July 11, 1788, George Clinton Papers, NYPL. For a similar speech by Patrick Henry, see Storing, *Complete Anti-Federalist*, 5:210–11.

27. "Speeches to the Delegates to Congress, 1786," Yates Papers, NYPL.

28. Storing, *Complete Anti-Federalist*, 6:109–10, 113.

29. *Debates*, June 20 and 21, 1788, 2:222–30, 243–51.

30. Storing, *Complete Anti-Federalist*, 2:281. Gilbert Livingston defended "equal

liberty" in the New York state ratifying convention. See *Debates*, June 24, 1788, 2:287. A group of prominent New York City Anti-Federalists, including Melancton Smith, declared themselves to be "friends of equal liberty." See "Minutes of the Society," November 4, 1788, Lamb Papers, NYHS.

31. Storing, *Complete Anti-Federalist*, 2:122.

32. "Rough Hewer" MSS, October 27, 1785, Yates Papers, NYPL. Yates transcribed this statement in his political papers even though he claimed not to be its author. The author assumed the pseudonym "Rough Hewer, Junior." Perhaps he was Abraham G. Lansing, Yates's son-in-law and political associate.

33. George Clinton's relentless pursuit of wealth is briefly discussed in E. Wilder Spaulding, *His Excellency George Clinton: Critic of the Constitution*, 2nd ed. (Port Washington, N.Y.: Ira J. Friedman, 1964), 228–31. For a perceptive account of how all three men's economic fortunes influenced their political thought, see Theophilus Parsons, Jr., "The Old Conviction versus The New Realities: New York Antifederalist Leaders and the Radical Whig Tradition" (Ph.D. diss., Columbia University, 1974), chap. 4, 8–9.

34. Spaulding, *His Excellency George Clinton*, 176–77; Smith to Yates, January 28, 1788, Yates Papers, NYPL. "Brutus" expressed a similar fear of "the powerful influence that great and designing men have over the honest and unsuspecting" (Storing, *Complete Anti-Federalist*, 2:284).

35. For a fine biography of Smith, see Robin Brooks, "Melancton Smith: New York Anti-Federalist, 1744–1798" (Ph.D. diss., University of Rochester, 1964).

36. [Melancton Smith], *An Address to the People of the State of New York: Showing the necessity of making Amendments to the Constitution, proposed for the United States, previous to its Adoption. By a Plebian.* (1788; Brooklyn, 1888), 21.

37. *Debates*, June 20, 1788, 2:227.

38. Ibid., 229–30.

39. Ibid., June 21, 1788, 2:248.

40. Ibid., 246–47.

41. Ibid., 257.

42. Ibid., June 23, 1788, 2:276.

43. Ibid., 277.

44. George Dangerfield, *Chancellor Robert R. Livingston of New York, 1746–1813* (New York: Harcourt, Brace, 1960), 228.

45. Ledlie to John Lamb, January 15, 1788, Lamb Papers, NYHS.

46. George Clinton to Lamb, June 28, 1788, Lamb Papers, NYHS.

47. DeWitt Clinton to Lamb, July 2, 1788, Lamb Papers, NYHS.

48. Rossiter, *Federalist Papers*, 214–15.

49. For Smith's speech concerning the Senate, see *Debates*, June 25, 1788, 2:309–15; for the "Federal Farmer," see Storing, *Complete Anti-Federalist*, 2:288.

50. *Debates*, June 24, 1788, 2:291–93.

51. Ibid., 301–03.

52. Dumbauld, *Bill of Rights*, 42–43.

53. *Debates*, June 24, 1788, 1:338–40.

54. Storing, *Complete Anti-Federalist*, 2:391.

55. Rossiter, *Federalist Papers*, no. 12, 296.

56. Max Farrand, ed., *The Records of the Federal Convention of 1787*, 2nd rev. ed. (New Haven, Conn.: Yale University Press, 1966), 2:655–57.

57. For the historical distinction between internal and external taxes, see Thomas P. Slaughter, *The Whiskey Rebellion: Frontier Epilogue to the American Revolution* (New York: Oxford University Press, 1986), chap. 1.

58. [Abraham Yates], *Political Papers, Addressed to the Advocates for a Congressional Revenue in the State of New-York* (New York, 1786), 13. The *Papers* reprinted some of the "Rough Hewer" and "Sidney" essays of 1785.

59. Thomas C. Cochran, *New York in the Confederation: An Economic Study* (1932; Clifton, N.J.: Augustus M. Kelley, 1972), chap. 7–9; Spaulding, *His Excellency George Clinton*, 153–78, 202. John Paul Kaminski, "Paper Politics: The Northern State Loan Officers during the Confederation, 1783–1790" (Ph.D. diss., University of Wisconsin, 1972), 21, 139–58.

60. Cochran, *New York in the Confederation*, p. 159.

61. *Debates*, June 28, 1788, 2:357–58; Spaulding, *His Excellency George Clinton*, 119–20.

62. Ibid., p. 359.

63. "Letters and Speeches," [July 17, 1788], Clinton Papers, NYPL.

64. Yates, "Political Papers," 8, 14–15. See also "Speeches to the Delegates," Yates Papers, NYPL. Yates's politics are indeed an extreme example of the widespread "jealousy of power" common during the revolutionary era. See James H. Hutson, "The Origins of 'the Paranoid Style in American Politics': Public Jealousy from the Age of Walpole to the Age of Jackson," in *Saints and Revolutionaries: Essays on Early American History*, ed. David D. Hall, John M. Murrin, and Thad W. Tate (New York: W. W. Norton, 1984), 332–72.

65. For biographical information on Yates, see Stephen Bielinski, *Abraham Yates, Jr., and the New Political Order in Revolutionary New York* (Albany: New York State American Revolution Bicentennial Commission, 1975); Parsons, "New York Anti-Federalist Leaders," chap. 4.

66. Staughton Lynd, "Abraham Yates's History of the Movement for the United States Constitution," *WMQ*, 3rd ser., 20 (April, 1963): 225.

67. Hamilton to Morris, August 13, 1782 in Harold C. Syrett, ed., *The Papers of Alexander Hamilton* (New York: Columbia University Press, 1962), 3:139.

68. Parsons, "New York Anti-Federalist Leaders," 150–57.

69. "Speeches to the Delegates," Yates Papers, NYPL.

70. Ibid. See also Yates, *Political Papers*.

71. "Rough Hewer" MSS, March 4, 1788, Yates Papers, NYPL. Caroline Robbins, "Algernon Sidney's *Discourses Concerning Government*: Textbook of Revolution," *WMQ*, 3rd ser., 4 (July, 1947): 267–96.

72. Ibid., December 8, 1788; Yates, *Political Papers*, 8.

73. Ibid. For Yates's use of historical sources, see Parsons, "New York Anti-Federalist Leaders," chap. 5.

74. Storing, *Complete Anti-Federalist*, 2:139.

75. "Speeches to the Delegates," Yates Papers, NYPL.

76. "Rough Hewer" MSS, January 27, 1794, Yates Papers, NYPL. See also Lynd, "Abraham Yates's History."

77. Smith, *An Address to the People of the State of New-York*.

78. Storing, *Complete Anti-Federalist*, 2:239–40, 388–400.

79. Ibid., 392–93.

80. Ibid.

81. *Debates*, June 27, 1788, 2:332–34.

82. Ibid., 350–52.

83. Ibid., 333.

84. Ibid., 1:322–23, 325–26, 329; 3:659. New York alone in 1788 passed the amendment on the excise. New York's proposal on direct federal taxation agreed with that of Massachusetts, South Carolina, and New Hampshire. Virginia adopted a somewhat different constitutional amendment on this issue.

85. Dumbauld, *Bill of Rights*, 43–44, 47.

86. Young, *Democratic-Republicans*, 177–83, 209; Dangerfield, *Chancellor Livingston*, 245–54; Spaulding, *His Excellency George Clinton*, chap. 22–24. Melancton Smith himself became a loyal Republican before his death in 1798 at the age of fifty-four. See Brooks, "Melancton Smith," p. 288.

87. Slaughter, *Whiskey Rebellion*, 226.

88. John C. Miller, *Crisis in Freedom: The Alien and Sedition Laws* (Boston: Little, Brown, 1951); Leonard W. Levy, *Jefferson and Civil Liberties: The Darker Side* (Cambridge, Mass.: Belknap Press, 1963), chap. 3.

89. *Debates*, June 24, 1788, 2:304–305. The strength of libertarian, states' rights concerns during the early national period is analyzed in Richard E. Ellis, "The Persistence of Antifederalism after 1789," in *Beyond Confederation*, ed. Beeman, Botein, and Carter, 295–314.

90. Storing, *Complete Anti-Federalist*, 2:387.

91. Hugh Ledlie to John Lamb, January 15, 1788, Lamb Papers, NYHS.

92. Yates, *Political Papers*, 8.

93. Storing, *Complete Anti-Federalist*, 2:117.

94. Rossiter, *Federalist Papers*, no. 1, 33; no. 11, 84–91; no. 23, 152–57.

95. Storing, *Complete Anti-Federalist*, 2:401.

96. Ibid., 5:219.

97. Micah 4:4. For the use of this passage by Smith and Henry, see *Plebian*, 6; Storing, *Complete Anti-Federalist*, 5:219.

RONALD L. HATZENBUEHLER

"Refreshing the Tree of Liberty with the Blood of Patriots and Tyrants": Thomas Jefferson and the Origins of the U.S. Constitution

IN NOVEMBER, 1986, a *Wall Street Journal*/NBC News poll asked a group of Americans to name the man who played the "biggest role" in drafting the Constitution. Not surprisingly, the majority answer was "Don't know." Thomas Jefferson was a close second (31 percent); only 1 percent of those sampled could correctly identify James Madison as the "Father of the Constitution."[1] Assuming that those who participated in the poll knew that Jefferson was the chief author of the Declaration of Independence, attributing the Constitution to him is understandable. That the Constitution was written by a committee defies logic.

Thomas Jefferson did not attend the Constitutional Convention; he was in France. More importantly, his initial statements concerning the Constitution contradicted some of the decisions of the men who wrote the document. Whereas such notables as George Washington, Alexander Hamilton, and James Madison believed that too much liberty in the hands of the states and people threatened national existence, Jefferson feared that excessive powers vested in the national government would destroy liberty and republican government. Instead of suggesting that the Articles of Confederation be replaced with a new document, Jefferson wrote to John Adams in November, 1788, that the "three or four" good aspects of the Constitution should have been "added to the good, old, and venerable fabrick, which should have been preserved even as a religious relique."[2]

In an extended, contemporaneous letter to Adams's son-in-law, William Stephens Smith, Jefferson charged that the Constitution threatened the people's right to resist tyranny. Rebellion, he cautioned, was always preferable to "lethargy, the forerunner of death to the public liberty";

> What country can preserve it's liberties if their rulers are not warned from time to time that their people preserve the spirit of resistance? Let them take arms. . . . What signify a few lives lost in a century or two? The tree of liberty must be refreshed from time to time with the blood of patriots and tyrants. It is its natural manure.[3]

How are we to explain such statements? Taken to their logical extent, Jefferson advocated not liberty but license. The best explanation for these thoughts, Jefferson's biographers agree, lies in his residency in Paris from 1784 through 1789. There, as Frenchmen moved toward a bloody revolution, Jefferson's language became increasingly inflammatory, perhaps even irrational. Instead of viewing American events in European terms, however, Jefferson responded to the Constitution in a manner that reflected his deeply felt biases concerning the conduct of politics in the United States. In fact, Jefferson formed his opinions of the Constitution based upon the meaning he assigned to Shays's Rebellion, not the French Revolution.

I

In 1951, two scholars stressed the impact of French society on Jefferson's opinions of the Constitution. "With fresh eyes from this new angle," Dumas Malone concluded, Jefferson gained a new perspective on America and further confirmed "his optimism about the American experiment." Some of Jefferson's friends in America hoped that the Constitution would save the nation from anarchy. Based upon his experience in France, Jefferson instead emphasized "the greater social peace of republican America than despotic Europe." Far from producing fears about the people's right to self-rule, Jefferson's "observations in Europe . . . served to quicken" his faith in American republicanism.[4]

Similarly, Nathan Schachner argued that European absolutism conditioned Jefferson's initial reactions to the Constitution. What struck him most forcefully were the problems that aristocrats and kings created for the peoples of Europe. Because his "firsthand [look at] the kings of Europe had made him almost pathologically fearful of the institution taking root in America," Jefferson strenuously opposed making the president reelectable, he fretted, for life.[5]

The biographies of Jefferson by Stuart Gerry Brown and Merrill D. Peterson, published in 1966 and 1971, respectively, and Lawrence S. Kaplan's 1967 monograph each correlated Jefferson's views of European tyranny with first impressions of the Constitution. Brown asserts that Jefferson's strident pronouncements about perpetual rebellion, vigilance against tyranny, and preservation of liberty can be understood only in the context of his stay in France. Following his return to America and especially as president, Jefferson expressed no further interest in having "a little rebellion now and then."[6] Peterson emphasizes that "viewed from Jefferson's European perch," turmoil in America during the 1780s "offered a not unpleasing picture of republican liberty flexing its muscles." Similarly, Jefferson's initial views of the Constitution — especially the absence of a bill of rights — were "founded on European rather than American fears."[7]

Kaplan's treatment of Jefferson in France is the most direct of all, noting an increase in Jefferson's extravagant use of language to describe events in America "as the tempo of the incipient French Revolution mounted." But Jefferson, greatly to his credit, never allowed his sympathy for the French Revolution to deflect his main goal of protecting and expanding American interests in France. In fact, the American minister favored constitutional monarchy for France "modeled on Great Britain's, but purged of British flaws" because he believed such a settlement would best benefit the United States. In this way, "the [French] Revolution had a far greater impact upon his opinions of events in America than it had upon his opinions of contemporaneous developments in France."[8]

In summary, these notable political biographies uniformly portray Jefferson's views of American events leading to the Constitution as reflections of his experiences in France. Consensus rules despite minor differences of emphasis.

But not totally. In 1984 Richard K. Matthews challenged notions of Jefferson "as a traditional eighteenth-century liberal." Jefferson's reaction to Shays's Rebellion and the Constitution, Matthews argues, was rooted in views of radical democracy, not prerevolutionary Parisian society. Matthews stresses Jefferson's uniqueness in American political history due to his espousal of perpetual, institutionalized revolution. In Jefferson's view, rebellions provided the opportunity for a new generation to create its own political community. Therefore, revolution was a cathartic, cleansing experience that kept "both humanity and society healthy, happy, and alive." Therefore, the *environment* within which Jefferson's thoughts emerged was immaterial. Whether in Virginia or France, "Jefferson was in exile among his own" because of his radical views about American society.[9]

Clearly, there is more at stake here than simply Jefferson's thoughts about the Constitution and the French Revolution. The central issues are consistency and context: Should Jefferson's statements about preserving liberty through periodic revolution be taken at face value or did he project his fears of French absolutism onto American politics? Were Jefferson's statements reactions to time and place or do they signify an open-ended commitment to revolution as the necessary prerequisite to preserving liberty? A close examinatioon of his commentary on American events from 1784 through 1789 helps to answer these questions.

II

When Thomas Jefferson left the United States for France on July 5, 1784, he had already developed significant political ideas and also had participated in many notable events. As a student at the College of William and Mary, he studied mathematics, natural history, and moral philosophy with the eminent Scottish teacher, William Small, and learned law from the prominent attorney, George Wythe. As a member of the House of Burgesses, he wrote at age thirty-one *A Summary View of the Rights of British America* — the pamphlet that established his credentials to write the Declaration of Independence. During the war, he served as a representative to the Continental Congress and from 1779 to 1781, as governor of Virginia during the British invasion of the state.

In spite of these accomplishments, Jefferson's life had not gone exactly as he might have planned. His father Peter, whose influence on Jefferson is more conjecture than fact, died when his eldest son was only fourteen years old. Various prospective mates slipped through his hands while he was in college and afterward, and he married Martha

Wayles Skelton on January 1, 1772, under circumstances that have left even his most sympathetic biographers perplexed.[10] As governor, the British invasion of Virginia caused Jefferson a score of problems, and immediately after his resignation Lt. Col. Banastre Tarleton nearly captured the entire Virginia Assembly in Charlottesville and Jefferson himself at Monticello. An official inquiry into Jefferson's conduct during this episode followed. The former governor was vindicated of all charges against him, but innuendoes of incompetency and cowardice haunted him for the rest of his life. Composing his *Notes on the State of Virginia* in the fall of 1781 must have helped Jefferson to forget his political problems, but Martha's death in September, 1782, was an especially heavy blow. Appointed to the peace mission later that year, he should have sailed to France in December, 1782, but weather delays and expectations of eventual peace with England in early 1783 scotched those plans. A second invitation in 1784 offered a respite from political controversy and personal tragedy. The especially fast passage (nineteen days) may have seemed portentous of good things to come during his stay in France.

From the beginning, the American minister's preferences for his native land over Europe were clear, especially in letters to younger correspondents. To James Monroe, he advised that a visit to Europe "will make you adore your own country, it's soil, it's climate, it's equality, liberty, laws, people and manners. My god! How little do my countrymen know what precious blessings they are in possession of, and which no other people on earth enjoy."[11] Neither did Europe possess any knowledge that Americans should want to learn. "Cast your eye over America," Jefferson advised a friend who asked advice about a European education. "Who are the men of most learning, of most eloquence, most beloved by their country and most trusted and promoted by them? They are those who have been educated among them, and whose manners, morals and habits are perfectly homogeneous with those of the country."[12]

With respect to France, his initial views are mostly those of a tourist — language was a problem;[13] finding suitable accommodations and clothing occupied his time;[14] and attending court functions presented numerous difficulties. Once he and his daughter Martha went to Versailles to view the queen at her entrance to the palace, but when the queen's coach arrived they could not see her. Next, they tried to view a military display and were shunted away by soldiers. "You can calculate," he wrote to John Adams, "the extent of mortification."[15]

While observing life in France and pressing American requests for additional trade opportunities, Jefferson informed himself about American affairs as best he could through his correspondents and American newspapers. In this way, he first learned of Shays's Rebellion and disorders in other New England states on December 11, 1786, courtesy of William S. Smith in London. In an accompanying letter, Smith informed Jefferson "of the expectation of a *General Indian* War and that Congress are raising troops on that ostensible Ground and for that ostensible reason." To Smith, the plan seemed flawed. "How they mean to employ 2 Companies of Dragoons of 120 Rank and File in this service I am not yet informed," he wrote.[16]

Jefferson did not respond to Smith until December 20, the same day that he received a lengthy letter from Secretary of Foreign Affairs John Jay. In contrast to what he had received from Smith, Jay's letter portrayed the rebellion in Massachusetts in the worst possible light. "A Spirit of Licentiousness," wrote Jay, "[produced by a] Reluctance to Taxes, and Impatience of Government, a Rage for Property, and little Regard to the Means of acquiring it, together with a Desire of Equality in all Things, seem to actuate the Mass of those who are uneasy in their Circumstances."

The problem with the rebellion, according to Jay, lay in the effect it would have on "the Minds of the rational and well intentioned." Because they would worry about their "Peace and Security, they will too naturally turn towards Systems in direct Opposition to those which oppress and disquiet them. If Faction should long bear down Law and Government, Tyranny may raise its Head, or the more sober part of the People may even think of a King."[17]

This letter must have greatly alarmed Jefferson; he mentioned it several times. In answer to Smith's letter, he said that he "first viewed the Eastern disturbances as of little consequence" until he received a letter (Jay's) that "represented them as serious." In like manner, Jefferson admitted to John Adams that "Mr. Jay's letter on the subject had really affected me" until he received one from Adams advising him not to be "allarmed at the late Turbulence in New England." Adams attributed the rebellion to a tax laid by the Massachusetts Assembly, a tax that was "rather heavier than the People could bear." Based on this letter, Jefferson assured members of the Adams family that he was no longer worried about the rebellion.[18]

After he overcame the initial shock of Jay's letter, Jefferson's thoughts on Shays's Rebellion seem to be organized around two primary foci. First, he placed this most recent event within strongly held attitudes relative to politics and society in New England in general and Massachusetts in particular. Cryptic but consistent comments in correspondence to friends and acquaintances from the area and to foreigners and Americans traveling abroad indicate Jefferson's basic orientation to life in Massachusetts. Secondly, as his concerns grew about the impact of Shays's Rebellion on the central government in the United States, he expanded his choice of correspondents and the scope of his concerns. When it appeared that Americans would overreact to Shays's Rebellion and strengthen the Articles of Confederation, Jefferson anticipated many dangers for his countrymen.

In his first letters to the Adamses in London and to Ezra Stiles, the president of Yale, Jefferson chose similar words to dismiss the implications of the rebellion. To John Adams he said, "I can never fear that things will go far wrong where common sense has fair play." To Abigail Adams, "Let common sense and common honesty have fair play and they will soon set things to rights." To Smith, "I hope . . . that the good sense of the people will be found the best army." Finally, to Stiles, "Let common sense and common honesty have fair play and they will soon set things to rights."[19]

For Jefferson, Massachusetts' problems were lodged not in the people but in the government. Although he did not detail the origins of his views on Massachusetts politics in 1786, attitudes he expressed later in his life were probably formed during the era of Shays's Rebellion or earlier. Writing to Adams in 1813, Jefferson distinguished between "a natural aristocracy . . . the grounds of which are virtue and talents" and an artificial aristocracy "founded on wealth and birth, without either virtue or talents." It was this latter group, Jefferson believed, that had dominated politics in Massachusetts since colonial days. By way of contrast, "in Virginia, we have nothing of this." From the earliest times, the electorate in Virginia had learned to discriminate between natural and pseudoaristocrats.

The other area where Virginian society was superior to that of Massachusetts concerned the power of the clergy in the two states. In

Massachusetts, a "strict alliance of church and state" prior to the American Revolution allowed ministers to attain a higher status than they deserved. In Virginia, however, the fixed salaries of clergymen, in Jefferson's view, discouraged rivalries and accumulation of riches, and thereby prevented their "acquiring influence over the people."[20] Virginia, therefore, was a land of tranquillity where men of virtue and talent rose to the top of society. In Massachusetts, however, the people had no recourse to liberty except through rebellion.

In explaining how government had gone wrong in Massachusetts in 1786, Jefferson turned primarily to newspapers and tried not to rely on information he received from those, like the Adamses, who had been infected by superstitions and heresies. From the newspapers, he concluded that the rebels were closing the courts because they did not have money to pay their foreign debts and taxes. Prior to the American Revolution, he reasoned, New Englanders had exported their whale oil and fish to England and the Mediterranean — the former closed in the 1780s by duties, the latter by pirates. Then, the Massachusetts Assembly, "in their zeal for paying their public debt had laid a tax too heavy to be paid in the circumstances of their state." He emphasized that the rebels had refrained from injury to persons or property and did not remain a day in any one place.[21]

Jefferson was undoubtedly trying to place the rebellion in the best possible light in order not to alarm his friends in other European countries, like C. W. F. Dumas at The Hague, or those who shared republican sympathies in France, like the Marquis de Lafayette. Nevertheless, two aspects of these letters deserve attention. First, many states in the nation had suspended the collection of debts during the American Revolution as a form of debtor relief. In contrast to Massachusetts, however, most southern states — including Virginia — did not reopen their courts until the 1790s. Throughout the period of Shays's Rebellion, Jefferson received letters from correspondents in Virginia and South Carolina ruing the day the courts reopened because of a fear of circumstances similar to those in New England.[22]

Most importantly, Jefferson correctly concluded from his newspapers that the citizens of Massachusetts were caught in a "chain of debt" stretching from London to Boston to Worcester and Springfield. Part of the problem involved a British rush after the war to dump surplus manufactured goods in the former colonies, but much of it was also due to zealous New England merchants who, anticipating demand for British goods to be high after the war, bought large amounts of goods on credit. Unfortunately, a depressed economy led to few purchases and a subsequent flow of specie to England to pay creditors.[23]

Jefferson did not fully understand this situation, but offered good advice to a friend in Boston in the summer of 1785 to beware of merchants in that area "who undertake to trade without capital; who therefore do not go to the market where commodities are to be had cheapest, but where they are to be had on the longest credit. The consumers pay for it in the end, and the debts contracted, and bankruptcies occasioned by such commercial adventurers, bring burthen and disgrace to our country."[24]

The theme of luxury and Americans' aping European tastes was a favorite of Jefferson's, and nowhere did he find more cause for alarm than in Boston. In the aftermath of rebellion, he wrote to Abigail Adams that "the disturbances in Massachusets are not yet at an end. Mr. Rucker . . . gives me a terrible account of the luxury of our ladies in the article of dress. He sais that they begin to be sensible of the excess of it themselves and think a reformation necessary. That proposed is the adoption of a national dress. I fear however they have not resolution enough for this."[25]

Fear of British involvement in the events surrounding Shays's Rebellion went far beyond credit problems and clothing fads, however. Jefferson sincerely believed, I am convinced, that Americans who wanted a stronger central government — and perhaps the English king again — planned to use Shays's Rebellion as their justification for constitutional change. In an extended letter in mid-January to Edward Carrington, the man he hoped to use in place of James Monroe as his mouthpiece and informant in the Confederation Congress, Jefferson compared the nature of government in America and in Europe. Those societies with minimal government, Jefferson argued, based their rights on public opinion, whereas all European governments, "under pretense of governing . . . [divide] their nations into two classes, wolves and sheep. I do not exaggerate. This is a true picture of Europe."[26]

One week later, he received a second letter from Jay deploring the fact that the Massachusetts government had treated the insurgents so lightly, blaming Great Britain for inciting Indians to warfare, and hoping that the British would not inflame the differences between eastern and western territories that surfaced in discussions over the Jay-Gardoqui Treaty.[27] On January 30, Jefferson repeated and embellished upon much of his letter to Carrington in one to Madison, but his mind was on Jay. "I hold it," Jefferson wrote in one of his most quoted passages, "that a little rebellion now and then is a good thing, and as necessary in the political world as storms in the physical." Governments should see that even the minor evil of volatility in the people produces much good—interest in and commitment to liberty. "Honest republican governors," therefore, should be "so mild in their punishment of rebellions, as not to discourage them too much." Then, immediately following this sentence: "If these transactions give me no uneasiness, I feel very differently at another piece of intelligence, to wit, the possibility that the navigation of the Missisipi may be abandoned to Spain."[28] Jay had misplaced his concerns, Jefferson thought. A rebellion in Massachusetts should not be allowed to create such an alarm, even when linked (erroneously, be believed) with British intrigue; and Jay should not exonerate his inept negotiations with such a lame excuse either.

Three days later, he received a letter from Abigail Adams in which she characterized Shays and his followers as "Ignorant, wrestless desperadoes, without conscience or principals, [who] have led a deluded multitude to follow their standard, under pretence of grievances which have no existance but in their immaginations." Taken one way, Jefferson's response to Abigail—"I like a little rebellion now and then. It is like a storm in the Atmosphere"—seems harsh and punitive. Rather, I think he was reacting to the second half of Abigail's letter wherein she expressed the belief that in spite of "much trouble and uneasiness" the rebellion would provoke "an investigation of the causes which have produced these commotions":

> Luxery and extravagance both in furniture and dress had pervaded all orders of our Countrymen and women, and was hastning fast to sap their independance by involving every class of citizens in distress, and accumulating debts upon them which they were unable to discharge. Vanity was becoming a more powerfull principal than patriotism. The lower order of the community were prest for taxes, and tho possest of landed property they were unable to answer the demand, whilst those who possest money were fearfull of lending, least the mad cry of the mob should force the Legislature upon a measure very different from the touch of Midas.

In spite of his penchant for repeating pithy statements to various correspondents, I question whether Jefferson would have used the "little rebellion" statement with Abigail unless he expected her to agree with him.[29] The extreme similarity in their views on part of the underlying causes of the rebellion must have led Jefferson to believe he could repeat to her the sentence he had used in Madison's letter. And when she reacted differently from his expectations — writing seldom and failing to discuss politics even when she did — Jefferson might have learned something. His other radical-sounding statement about Shays's Rebellion — that the tree of liberty needed refreshing periodically with the blood of patriots and tyrants — appeared only once in his letters.

III

The main point so far in this discussion of Jefferson's initial reactions to Shays's Rebellion is that he probably felt Massachusetts deserved what had happened. If the state were purged of aristocratic families and ministers who acted like priests, the people themselves could be reformed and thereby remove the need for rebellions. But there was another, deeper problem inherent in Shays's Rebellion contained in both Jay's and Adams's first letters to Jefferson about the revolt. Both men expected the rebellion, in Adams's words, to "terminate in additional Strength to Government."[30]

From his first accounts of Shays's Rebellion, Jefferson worried that the revolt in Massachusetts would lead to the formation of a stronger central government in the United States. As citizens of the most populous and wealthy state in the union, Virginians were confident that their state could handle affairs without outside interference. Indeed, the chief reason for Virginia's active involvement in revolutionary events after 1774 had been the fear that England would overturn Burgesses' control of Virginia's affairs.[31] As governor, Jefferson had felt the need for a more concerted action on the part of the states in meeting the wartime needs of the country, and as minister to France he came to believe that a stronger union of the states would improve the conduct of foreign policy. But these attitudes never influenced his views on domestic affairs. If Jay and the Confederation Congress were able to raise an army to suppress an internal convulsion in Massachusetts under the guise of an Indian war, what would prevent disturbances in other states from provoking a similar response, or worse, of creating a more powerful central government over the states?

By mid-June, Jefferson had heard from Madison, Franklin, and other valued correspondents that Shays's Rebellion had ended peaceably, with pardons for the participants and the election of a new governor.[32] Thus, he was able to write the last chapter of this part of the story in a letter to David Hartley, an American residing in England. The causes of the rebellion, Jefferson modestly opined, were internal to Massachusetts and revolved around an inability to pay debts. "I believe you may be assured," Jefferson wrote more confidently, "that an idea or desire of returning to any thing like their antient government never entered into their heads." Then, some quantitative evidence: one insurrection in thirteen states in eleven years meant that any single state could expect only one rebellion every 143 years! Far from providing an example of instability in American government, Shays's Rebellion proved how inherently stable the American republic was.[33]

As Jefferson began to receive reports concerning the convening of the Constitutional Convention in Philadelphia, his views changed. In mid-July he received a letter from Madison containing a list of delegates meeting in Philadelphia and a lengthy discussion of the impression John Adams's *Defence of the Constitutions of the United States of America* was having on those same delegates. Madison feared that the book would further incline those from eastern states toward "the British Constitution" and prove to be "a powerful engine in forming the public opinion."[34] By August, Jefferson was seriously entertaining the prospect that some Americans would prefer monarchical to republican government. He also considered lobbying those men meeting in Philadelphia to make "one nation in every case concerning foreign affairs, and separate ones in whatever is merely domestic." States should be made to execute national laws (especially payments on the national debt), he felt, but this pressure should be light and "peaceable."[35]

Sometime in early November, he saw the Constitution for the first time, courtesy of John Adams.[36] Again, his first reactions provide important clues to his attitudes. Writing to Adams, Jefferson immediately railed against the powers of the executive officer. Characterizing the president as "a bad edition of a Polish king" because he could be re-elected every four years for life, Jefferson prophesied that the office would at every election be "worthy of intrigue, of force, and even of foreign interference. It will be of great consequence to France and England to have America governed by a Galloman or an Angloman."[37] He repeated the same ideas to William S. Smith, but as before he wrote with more emphasis. First, he blamed the British for "impudent and persevering lying" regarding the instability of government under the Articles of Confederation:

> The British ministry have so long hired their gazetteers to repeat and model into every form lies about our being in anarchy, that the world has at length believed them, the English nation had believed them, the ministers themselves have come to believe them, and what is more wonderful, we have believed them ourselves. Yet where does this anarchy exist? Where did it ever exist, except in a single instance of Massachusets?

Then follows a repeat of his calculations about the number of revolutions per state per year, and the statement about blood being the "natural manure" of the tree of liberty. "Our Convention," he wrote, "has been too much impressed by the insurrection in Massachusets; and in the spur of the moment they are setting up a kite to keep the hen yard in order."[38] Jefferson's worse fears had now materialized — rebellion in Massachusetts threatened liberty nationwide because national leaders had panicked.

By December, 1787, Jefferson settled on the addition of a bill of rights as the best way to ameliorate the problems he saw in too much control vested in the national government and the president.[39] Ironically, this suggestion appears to have come from John Adams, for Jefferson does not mention it prior to receiving Adams's letter on November 26. In this letter, Adams asked Jefferson, "What think you of a Declaration of Rights? Should not such a thing have preceded the Model?"[40]

Jefferson's modification of his views on a bill of rights reinforces the view that Adams's suggestion spurred Jefferson's interest in amending the Constitution. At first, Jefferson wanted no state to ratify the document without the amendments;[41] next he favored having four states make their ratification contingent on the changes;[42] finally he promoted a swift ratification with the subsequent passage of amendments.[43] It was the precarious financial situation of the government in Europe (his personal credit inextricably entwined with the nation's) that caused him to change his mind so many times. As the nation's credit sank, Jefferson's obstructionism disappeared.[44] Finally, on July 18, Jefferson wrote to Edward Rutledge that Americans "can surely boast of having set the world a beautiful example of a government reformed by reason alone without bloodshed."[45]

While Jefferson was accommodating himself to the American Constitution and forgetting about Daniel Shays and his "little rebellion," the French were rushing toward revolution. Despite growing unrest throughout France in 1788, however, Jefferson repeatedly referred to Louis XVI in terms such as "the honestest man in his kingdom, and the most regular and oeconomical," or as the one person in the country most favorable toward liberty for his people.[46] In direct contrast to his views of Daniel Shays and the New England revolts in general, Jefferson expressed no sympathy for mob behavior under any circumstances. Even bread riots in May, 1789, that left over a hundred persons dead provoked the observation that "the wretches know not what they wanted, except to do mischief. [The riot] seems to have had no particular connection with the great national questions now in agitation." To Madison he reported that the suppression of the riots "has been universally approved, as they seemed to have no view but mischief and plunder."[47]

IV

Although the two events are contemporaneous, Shays's Rebellion and the French Revolution have few similarities. Shays's Rebellion emerged from a period of economic dislocation following the American Revolution. It evoked remarkable restraint on the part of rebels and government and led to economic and political reforms in Massachusetts. The causes, course, and consequences of the French Revolution were far more dramatic for French society. Shays's Rebellion marked an increase in the *rate* of change in the communities of western Massachusetts, but it produced neither discontinuous nor transforming changes in society. The French Revolution, by way of contrast, severely weakened aristocratic authority in the nation and stimulated republicanism — a change in the *direction* of change. In short, the French Revolution was revolutionary; Shays's Rebellion was not.[48]

The American minister to France, however, reversed the importance of the two events. Jefferson's biographers have badly overstated his commitment to the French Revolution and depreciated his interest in Shays's Rebellion. Jefferson deliberately downplayed radicalism while he was in France because he feared that Americans would lose their French sympathies and that the English would use French instability to destroy American independence.[49] When the "blood of tyrants" flowed in torrents in France, Jefferson was safely back in the United States, serving as secretary of state. He continued to feel sympathy for the French people and nation, but he never repeated his radical-sounding statements about blood providing a natural manure for liberty trees after he left France in 1789. In Paris and throughout his life, he successfully separated American and French politics.

As for Shays's Rebellion, Jefferson tried to place the event in the best possible light because of fears that American leaders might go too far in strengthening the national government. He used excessive language in letters to close friends to warn them not to project the New England events onto American society as a whole. And when the Constitutional Convention met, he cautioned Madison, Washington, and other Virginia delegates not to allow the Massachusetts problems to undermine liberty in Virginia. Shays's Rebellion could occur only, Jefferson reasoned, in a state like Massachusetts where clergy and aristocratic families stifled freedom. Far away from his home, Jefferson used this "little rebellion" to warn Virginians not to trade their liberty for the illusive dream of "a more perfect union."

NOTES

1. In candor, 1 percent may be inflated if projected across American society as a whole. See *Wall Street Journal*, November 28, 1986, pp. A1 and A7.

2. Thomas Jefferson to John Adams, 13 November 1787, *The Papers of Thomas Jefferson*, ed. Julian Boyd et al., 20 vols. (Princeton: Princeton University Press, 1950–   ), 12:351. Hereafter cited as *Papers*. Jefferson's spelling and that of his correspondents is retained throughout this essay, as they appear in *Papers*.

3. Thomas Jefferson to William S. Smith, 13 November 1787, ibid., 356.

4. Dumas Malone, *Jefferson and His Time: Jefferson and the Rights of Man* (Boston: Little, Brown, 1951), 153–66.

5. Nathan Schachner, *Thomas Jefferson: A Biography* (reprint, New York: Thomas Yoseloff, 1957), 346–47.

6. Stuart G. Brown, *Thomas Jefferson* (New York: Washington Square Press, 1966), 220–23.

7. Merrill D. Peterson, *Thomas Jefferson and the New Nation: A Biography* (New York: Oxford University Press, 1970), 359–60.

8. Lawrence S. Kaplan, *Jefferson and France: An Essay on Politics and Political Ideas* (New Haven, Conn.: Yale University Press, 1967), 24–36.

9. Richard K. Matthews, *The Radical Politics of Thomas Jefferson: A Revisionist View* (Lawrence: University Press of Kansas, 1984), 15, 86, 117–26.

10. See, e.g., Malone, *Jefferson the Virginian*, 155–60. For an alternative view, see Page Smith, *Jefferson: A Revealing Biography* (New York: American Heritage Publishing Co., 1976), 56–60.

11. Thomas Jefferson to James Monroe, 17 June 1785, *Papers*, 8:223.

12. Thomas Jefferson to John Barrister, Jr., 15 October 1785, ibid., 637.

13. Thomas Jefferson to William S. Smith, 22 June 1785, ibid., 249.

14. Thomas Jefferson to James Monroe, 11 November 1784, ibid., 7:512.

15. Thomas Jefferson to John Adams, 25 May 1785, ibid., 8:164.

16. William S. Smith to Thomas Jefferson, 5 December 1786, ibid., 10:578.

17. John Jay to Thomas Jefferson, 27 October 1786, ibid., 488–89.

18. Thomas Jefferson to William S. Smith, 5 December 1786, ibid., 578; John Adams to Thomas Jefferson, 30 November 1786, ibid., 557; Thomas Jefferson to John Adams, 20 December 1785, ibid., 619; Thomas Jefferson to Abigail Adams, 21 December 1785, ibid., 621.

19. Ibid.; Thomas Jefferson to Ezra Stiles, 24 December 1786, ibid., 629.

20. Thomas Jefferson to John Adams, 18 October 1813, in Lester J. Cappon, ed., *The Adams-Jefferson Letters*, 2 vols. (Chapel Hill: University of North Carolina Press, 1959), 2:388–89.

21. Thomas Jefferson to C. W. F. Dumas, 25 December 1786, *Papers*, 10:631; Thomas Jefferson to William Carmichael, 26 December 1786, ibid., 633–34; Thomas Jefferson to Edward Carrington, 16 January 1787, ibid., 48–50.

22. Emory G. Evans, "Private Indebtedness and the Revolution in Virginia," *William and Mary Quarterly*, 3rd ser., 19 (1962): 511–33; David Ramsay to Thomas Jefferson, 8 November 1786, *Papers*, 10:513, and 7 April 1787, ibid., 11:279; Alexander Donald to Thomas Jefferson, 1 March 1787, ibid., 11:194.

23. David P. Szatmary, *Shays' Rebellion: The Making of an Agrarian Insurrection* (Amherst: University of Massachusetts Press, 1980), 1–33.

24. Thomas Jefferson to Nathaniel Tracy, 17 August 1785, *Papers*, 8:398.

25. Thomas Jefferson to Abigail Adams, 30 August 1787, ibid., 12:65.

26. Thomas Jefferson to Edward Carrington, 16 January 1787, ibid., 11:49.

27. John Jay to Thomas Jefferson, 14 December 1786, ibid., 10:596–99.

28. Thomas Jefferson to James Madison, 30 January 1787, ibid., 11:93.

29. Abigail Adams to Thomas Jefferson, 29 January 1787, ibid., 86; Thomas Jefferson to Abigail Adams, 22 February 1787, ibid., 174–75. A different interpretation of the discussion on "luxury" can be found in Phyllis Lee Levin, *Abigail Adams: A Biography* (New York: St. Martin's Press, 1987), 235–36.

30. John Adams to Thomas Jefferson, 30 November 1786, *Papers*, 10:557.

31. Jack P. Greene, "Society, Ideology, and Politics: An Analysis of the Political Culture of Mid-Eighteenth Century Virginia," in Richard M. Jellison, ed., *Society, Freedom, and Conscience: The Coming of the Revolution in Virginia, Massachusetts, and New York* (New York: Norton, 1976), 14–76.

32. William Short to Thomas Jefferson, 26 March 1787, *Papers*, 11:239–42; James Madison to Thomas Jefferson, 23 April 1787, ibid., 307; Benjamin Franklin to Thomas Jefferson, 19 April 1787, ibid., 301–2.

33. Thomas Jefferson to David Hartley, 2 July 1787, ibid., 526.

34. James Madison to Thomas Jefferson, 6 June 1787, ibid., 400–402.

35. Thomas Jefferson to Benjamin Hawkins, 4 August 1787, ibid., 684. See also Thomas Jefferson to David Ramsay, 4 August 1787, ibid., 687; Thomas Jefferson to William Hay, 4 August 1787, ibid., 685; Thomas Jefferson to John Blair, 13 August 1787, ibid., 12:28; and Thomas Jefferson to George Washington, 14 August 1787, ibid., 36.

36. John Adams to Thomas Jefferson, 10 November 1787, 12:335.

37. Thomas Jefferson to John Adams, 13 November 1787, ibid., 350.

38. Thomas Jefferson to William S. Smith, 13 November 1787, ibid., 356.

39. Thomas Jefferson to James Madison, 20 December 1787, ibid., 439–42. Ironically, Madison also was trying to save Virginia's status as the most powerful state in the nation by working for a new Constitution. Madison feared that without a change in the Articles, other states would force Virginians to pay their back money on the national debt and perhaps produce a document even stronger than the Constitution. See Lance G. Banning, "James Madison and the Nationalists, 1780–1783," *William and Mary Quarterly*, 3rd ser., 40 (1983): 227–55; idem, "The Hamiltonian Madison: A Reconsideration," *Virginia Magazine of History and Biography*, 92 (1984): 3–28.

40. John Adams to Thomas Jefferson, 10 November 1787, ibid., 12:335.

41. Thomas Jefferson to John Adams, 13 November 1787, ibid., 350; Thomas Jefferson to James Madison, 20 December 1787, ibid., 441.

42. Thomas Jefferson to William S. Smith, 2 February 1788, ibid., 558; Thomas Jefferson to James Madison, 6 February 1788, ibid., 567–70; Thomas Jefferson to Alexander Donald, 7 February 1788, ibid., 571.

43. Thomas Jefferson to William Carmichael, 3 June 1788, ibid., 13:232–33; Thomas Jefferson to Thomas Lee Shippen, 19 June 1788, ibid., 277; Thomas Jefferson to John Brown Cutting, 8 July 1788, ibid., 315–16.

44. See esp. Thomas Jefferson to John Jay, 13 March 1788, ibid., 12:661; Thomas Jefferson to George Washington, 2 May 1788, ibid., 13:125–28; and Thomas Jefferson to John Brown, 28 May 1788, ibid., 212. Although not directly related to the subject of this paper, I believe that Jefferson's personal debts were the primary stimulus for his "the earth belongs always to the living generation" letter to James Madison, 6 September 1789, ibid., 391–98.

45. Thomas Jefferson to Edward Rutledge, 18 July 1788, ibid., 378. Similarly, he reported to C. W. F. Dumas on 30 July 1788, "I think the internal affairs of this country will be settled without bloodshed" (ibid., 336). See also Thomas Jefferson to John Adams, 2 August 1788, ibid., 455.

46. Thomas Jefferson to John Brown Cutting, 23 August 1788, ibid., 538; Thomas Jefferson to William Short, 21 November 1788, ibid., 14:276.

47. Thomas Jefferson to William Carmichael, 8 May 1789, ibid., 15:104; Thomas Jefferson to John Jay, 9 May 1789, ibid., 110; Thomas Jefferson to James Madison, 11 May 1789, ibid., 121; and Thomas Jefferson to John Rutledge, Jr., 18 September 1789, ibid., 452–53.

48. This definition of "revolutionary change" is borrowed from David Hackett Fischer, *Growing Old in America* (New York: Oxford University Press, 1977), 100.

49. Kaplan, *Jefferson and France*, 36; and "Jefferson and the Constitution: The View from Paris," *Diplomatic History* 11 (1987): 323.

MICHAEL KAMMEN

Personal Liberty and American Constitutionalism

THE HISTORY of liberty in American thought and culture is endlessly enigmatic yet intriguing. Part of the fascination lies in the fact that liberty has meant different things to different persons, depending upon the period and its circumstances. Several years ago I developed a schematization for comprehending the history of liberty in American life. It emphasized the distinctive way that we have tended to conceptualize liberty at any given time in relation to other essential attributes or qualities in our political culture. Consequently, I stressed the tension between liberty and authority in the age of colonization; liberty and property during the eighteenth century; the dialectic of liberty and order for the nineteenth; and liberty and justice in our own era. I concluded that liberty and equality—a linkage that has long been problematic and precarious—might very well become the determinative nexus for liberty in the years ahead.[1]

Throughout my research I encountered various particular applications of the concept of liberty, such as natural liberty, civil liberty, political liberty, and liberty of conscience. Defining each of those phrases presented no problem, because the writers who employed them were usually quite explicit. And wherever authors failed to define their terms fully, a careful look at context would invariably solve the problem. One variation eluded me, however, because its usage seemed so protean and vague. At any given moment, even, different persons meant different things when they invoked the notion of "personal liberty." Nevertheless, the concept turns up with such frequency from the age of the founders to our own time that for me it became a special challenge and a personal agenda, as it were, to track and identify what appeared to be the most elusive single facet of the history of liberty in American constitutional thought: the notion of personal liberty.

(I might add that this project became all the more enticing, yet frustrating and daunting as well, whenever I had the following sort of conversation with distinguished judges or constitutional experts: "In the course of your work, do you often run across the phrase 'personal liberty'?" "Yes, in fact, I do." "Can you tell me anything specific about its meaning, either historically or in modern usage?" "Golly! No, I really can't. That's a very nebulous notion, isn't it? I mean truly slippery, don't you think so?" "Yes," I would have to reply, "I surely do.")

My mission in this essay, therefore, is an attempt to fill a fairly curious gap in our constitutional and cultural history. The reader will find that the meaning of personal liberty has evolved historically — which hardly should surprise anyone. We also learn that, at any given time, the notion of personal liberty has been relied upon by radicals, moderates, and conservatives — even though customarily each group attached its own particular meaning or interpretation to the phrase.

Finally, I find that in a very real sense personal liberty has been a concept that has not one, but two, fairly concrete connotations during the age of the American Revolution. Subsequently the concept became a curious catchall. Without anyone quite intending it to happen, personal liberty came to be used very casually and carried quite disparate meanings. (It could also be invoked in ways that were utterly meaningless.) Since the 1950s, however, from the era when communist witch-hunts were commonplace through the sexual revolution (with an increasing premium being placed upon the "right" of privacy), personal liberty has been transformed from a sometimes vapid omnium-gatherum to a meaningful aspect of discourse about values that many Americans now hold very dear. Personal liberty in 1987 did not mean quite what it meant in 1787. The nature of its transformation reveals much about the history of American values during the past two centuries.

I

It seems appropriate, and I hope more instructive than confusing, to begin with the vexing vagaries of the concept. There has been a tendency for public figures, when obliged to deliver an address on ceremonial and commemorative occasions, or even in politically controversial situations, to refer to personal liberty without defining it or providing a sufficient texture that might clarify its meaning in the particular context at hand. That was the case when Charles Evans Hughes addressed the annual meeting of the American Bar Association in 1925 ("our cherished traditions of personal liberty"); when Franklin Delano Roosevelt delivered a radio fireside chat right after the announcement of his "court-packing" plan in 1937 ("the present attempt by those opposed to progress to play upon the fears of danger to personal liberty"); and when Lewis F. Powell, president of the American Bar Association in 1965, spoke at Runnymede in ceremonies honoring the 750th anniversary of Magna Charta.[2]

Serious works by modern students of American culture and constitutionalism are more likely to use the phrase casually than precisely.[3] Contemporary journalism rarely bothers to define the term. Thus the *Nation*'s lead editorial in June, 1986, expressed concern because the Supreme Court seemed to be moving in a conservative direction: "Its rulings on personal liberty and equality reach into every corner of our national life, from abortion to affirmative action."[4] And throughout the nineteenth century writers were likely to use such phrases as "individual liberty" and "personal freedom" in a manner that seemed synonymous with personal liberty.[5]

Americans engaged by constitutional issues during the later 1780s might on occasion refer to "public liberty," which implied the existence of a complementary type that might be designated as personal liberty.[6] In *The Federalist* (no. 10), James Madison did provide a separation between "public and personal liberty." Whereas the former apparently referred to the right to vote, hold office, and assemble peacefully, the latter (also referred to as "private rights") seems to have subsumed freedom of worship, expression, and physical movement. Later in the same paper Madison also condemned pure democracies as being incompatible with "personal security, or the rights of property."[7]

In those few, brief phrases he came closest to revealing what the founders meant by personal liberty. Using a classic dichotomy of political philosophy, they differentiated between positive and negative liberty. For purposes of our inquiry, that meant understanding public liberty as *freedom to* do something and personal liberty as *freedom from* some act of intervention or encroachment, particularly by government.[8] Only on occasion, however, did subsequent writers sustain this distinction between public and private (or personal) liberty during the nineteenth century.[9]

The dissent written by Justice Joseph P. Bradley in the famous *Slaughter-House Cases* (1873), however, is noteworthy for our purposes because he traced all the way back to Magna Charta the right of habeas corpus, or "the right of having any invasion of personal liberty judicially examined into, at once, by a competent judicial magistrate. Blackstone classifies these fundamental rights under three heads, as the absolute rights of individuals, to wit: the right of personal security, the right of personal liberty, and the right of private property."[10] Bradley thereby leads us quite appropriately back to the British origins of the quarry we seek.

II

Blackstone is, indeed, the most relevant British writer. In his *Commentaries on the Laws of England* (1765–69) he ranked personal security among "the absolute rights of individuals"; but when he referred to personal liberty per se, he simply meant "the power of locomotion, of changing situation." Precisely because *we* now take for granted freedom of the person from physical restraint, an act of historical imagination is required in order to understand that in medieval and early modern times such a right could not be taken for granted at all. Although it was protected, in theory, by the 39th Article of Magna Charta, by statutes passed during the reign of King Edward III, and by common law, subjects recognized its vulnerability.[11]

Blackstone is also important as the primary agent of intellectual transmission to the world of the framers. When James Wilson of Pennsylvania touched upon personal liberty in his *Lectures on Law* (1790), he cited Blackstone as his authority. The same is true of Timothy Dwight of Connecticut, who in 1794 distinguished repeatedly between the right of private property, the right of personal security (against physical harm), and the right of personal liberty (physical mobility); he, too, cited Blackstone as his authority. It is noteworthy, however, that whereas Blackstone designated all these as "civil liberties," Americans preferred to regard them as natural rights.[12] That emphasis would reappear in language used by Justice William O. Douglas during the 1950s and 1960s.

Prior to making a permanent transatlantic transition, however, we should notice two other (pre-Blackstone) elements in the British background to our story. The first is secular, and the second might be termed spiritual.

Concerning the first: infringements of personal liberty (physical restraint) provided the principal complaint lodged in the Petition of Right of 1627. Those deep hostilities that deteriorated into tragic civil war during the 1640s elicited some public polemics involving personal liberty—though ultimately a total impasse developed between Royalists and Roundheads. Parliament passed the Habeas Corpus Act of 1679 solely to protect personal liberty against crown usurpation.[13] The most important legacy to the colonists from seventeenth-century England, however, came from John Locke—and it came to them as an assertion that one's personal freedom could be constrained only if due process of law had been observed.[14]

Concerning the second: during the middle decades of the seventeenth century, when the English civil war engendered so much ferment in customary political thought, the Puritan cause nourished a new concern for what its advocates called Christian liberty. The immediate implication was a belief in the equality of all believers. But John Milton anticipated its long-term impact by placing the concept of Christian liberty at the very core of his rationale for religious toleration. Although the Presbyterians and Independents differed over nuances, they both believed in freedom of conscience as the birthright of a Christian. Eventually the doctrine of Christian liberty would be used to sustain campaigns for religious freedom.[15] Young John Locke, writing his first philosophical treatises in 1660–61, elaborated that outlook, and it subsequently came to fruition in 1689 in the Act of Toleration.[16]

Those Puritans who immigrated to New England carried with them John Milton's concept of Christian liberty. They had not yet read Milton, nor did they really need to; for their views were formed in the very same crucible of experience that shaped Milton's. John Winthrop reflected upon Christian "libertie" before he ever left England; and the concept would be formalized in 1641 when the Massachusetts Bay Colony promulgated its Body of Liberties.[17]

John Wise, a third-generation Puritan clergyman who lived in Ipswich, Massachusetts, published a defense of congregational church government in 1717 in which he insisted that an individual's "Personal

Liberty and Equality [are] to be cherished, and preserved to the highest degree." Twenty-seven years later Elisha Williams published in Boston *The Essential Rights and Liberties of Protestants*, an appeal for liberty of conscience that ran in direct line of descent from John Milton's assertions a century earlier. Williams described Christian liberty as "the most valuable of all our rights," and connected it to the privilege of private judgment.[18]

Elisha Williams (1694–1755) cannot be described as a typical writer of his age. During the first half of the eighteenth century, he spoke for a vocal minority, but an articulate group highly aware that its avant garde ideas derived some legitimacy from Milton and Locke. During the 1770s and 1780s, though, their legacy entered the mainstream of American thought, with the result that the revolutionary generation was most likely to identify personal liberty as freedom of conscience. They took care to differentiate between "civil liberties and those of religion"; and it is clear from their language that civil liberties were essentially political (freedom to) whereas "ecclesiastical liberties" were essentially personal (freedom from).[19]

Coming upon the American scene during the 1830s, Tocqueville listened to accounts of those distinctions — by then blurred in a society swept by evangelical impulses — and misunderstood the language of liberty as it had been used by the revolutionary generation: "For the Americans the ideas of Christianity and liberty are so completely mingled that it is almost impossible to get them to conceive of the one without the other." Tocqueville's generalization *did* convey the "climate of opinion" during the 1830s, however, and thereby serves as a measure of American drift toward total imprecision in the use of liberty as a cultural concept.[20]

III

When we shift from the Anglo-American ideal of Christian liberty — which clearly developed into the doctrine of liberty of conscience (one of the major connotations of personal liberty in the eighteenth century) — to more secular aspects of American political culture during the revolutionary generation, we encounter a growing concern that emerged after the 1750s. In 1775, for example, the author of a letter written to a Massachusetts newspaper declared that "personal liberty, personal security and private property are the only motives" that explain why persons abandon a state of nature and willingly place themselves under government.[21]

Property in this instance means just what it says, of course; and security refers to possible physical harm and to the protection of one's home. Personal liberty, as usual, is not entirely clear. It *could* refer to freedom of conscience; but comparable statements from the period suggest either a Blackstonian sense of freedom from restraint, or the right to be a "free" person in the commonly understood Lockean sense of that day,[22] or even an embryonic form of what Justice Douglas would call, almost two centuries later, the right to be let alone and to have that right respected as well as protected by the government.

In 1787–88, however, Americans not only mentioned personal liberty with greater frequency, but they also began to use the phrase with increasing specificity. No one would deny that Montesquieu was the most persistently cited political philosopher when the federal Constitution came to be written and ratified. Although he alluded to "liberty of the subject" in *The Spirit of the Laws*, Montesquieu's emphasis was upon political liberty and physical security.[23]

By contrast, when Gouverneur Morris spoke critically in the Constitutional Convention of abuses by state legislatures during the 1780s, he specified "excesses agst. personal liberty, private property, & personal safety."[24] James Wilson would reinforce that sort of tripartite differentiation;[25] but, perhaps predictably, it would be James Madison (in a neglected passage from *The Federalist* [no. 10] who commented upon a growing concern for "public and personal liberty," and then noted the "prevailing and increasing distrust of public engagements, and alarm for private rights, which are echoed from one end of the continent to the other."[26]

How helpful it would be if we could know just what James Madison meant by the phrases "personal liberty" and "private rights." I do not claim to know for certain; but there are two essential clues. The first comes in Madison's own words, spoken at the Convention, when he declared that "a man has property in his opinions and the free communication of them, he has property in the free use of his faculties, in the safety and liberty of his person."[27]

The second clue is deductive. In 1789 Madison prepared for the first United States Congress the Bill of Rights that so many persons, Federalists as well as Anti-Federalists, had pleaded for in 1787–88. There is reason to believe that bills of attainder, ex post facto laws, and other such abhorrent legal actions were viewed as unwarranted violations of personal liberty.[28]

How helpful it would be, as well, if we could conclude that by 1787–89 some sort of consensus had been achieved concerning the meaning of personal liberty. That did not happen, however, and various sorts of incantations were uttered. Although they all are symptomatic and unexceptionable in their own way, they do not cohere into a pattern. Samuel Chase, the prominent Anti-Federalist from Maryland, opposed "the proposed national government, because it *immediately* takes away the power from our *state* legislature to protect the *personal* liberty of the citizen."[29]

Late in 1788 Thomas Jefferson wrote to George Washington from Paris that Lafayette had fallen "out of favor with the court, but [is] high in favor with the nation. I once feared for his personal liberty. But I hope him on safe ground at present." Finally, it is believed that the title preferred by Washington was "His High Mightiness, the President of the United States and Protector of their Liberties."[30] It is unclear whether the liberties he had in mind were those of the states or those of persons. Perhaps the ambiguity was not accidental, but rather a means of mollifying the fears of men like Samuel Chase.

In any case, as the eighteenth century drew to a close, James Wilson would make the most acute summary judgment: "In some respects, private liberty is still the orphan neglected."[31]

IV

The decades from 1790 until 1865 — from the end of the revolutionary era until the close of the Civil War — did very little to refine or clarify American conceptions of personal liberty. Complaints voiced by artisans and small shopkeepers indicated that Wilson's lament remained valid. As one perplexed individual wrote in New York City: "If a man seeks credit, he does not pledge his *personal* liberty for payment."[32] That grievance, uttered in 1811, would not be resolved until another generation had passed. Imprisonment for debt became an exceedingly controversial issue among reformers during the Jacksonian era.

So far as the United States Supreme Court and state supreme courts were concerned, personal liberty received scant illumination. When it was referred to at all, the concept seemed to reflect its most conventional implication: freedom from physical restraint.[33] Presidential messages to Congress and inaugural addresses occasionally included the phrase; but it meant somewhat different things in different situations — when it meant anything at all. In 1825 John Quincy Adams seemed to use it as a euphemism for economic individualism and opportunity. William Henry Harrison conveyed the same sense as the justices cited above; and John Tyler, after reassuring Southerners that the Constitution would be upheld, promised with meaningless vagueness that personal liberty would be "placed beyond hazard or jeopardy."[34]

Because Tyler was decidedly unsympathetic to the antislavery movement, his incantation may seem oddly inappropriate. We too easily forget the casuistry and half-truths that characterized American discourse concerning slavery between the Revolution and the Civil War. David Ramsay, for instance, the Philadelphian transplanted to South Carolina, offered this platitudinous paradox in 1789: "All masters of slaves who enjoy personal liberty will be both proud and jealous of their freedom."[35]

The most important development during this period, for the concept that we have under consideration, involved the passage by Northern states of personal liberty laws designed to challenge and undermine the Fugitive Slave Laws of 1793 and 1850. Although the history of that movement has been carefully analyzed,[36] we should at least note that pamphleteers were responsible for a new wrinkle that set them apart from the revolutionary generation. They tended to conflate, rather than differentiate between, civil and personal liberty. As Noah Porter, the president of Yale, put it in 1856: "Civil liberty implies firm guarantees of personal liberty." The guarantees provided by our form of government, he continued, were threefold: the principle that a man's home is his castle, the constitutional protection against general warrants, and the Habeas Corpus Act.[37]

Once the Civil War got under way and emergency war powers took effect, the primary locus of meaning for personal liberty shifted from legal protection for fugitive slaves and free blacks to the problem of habeas corpus and President Lincoln's perceived abuse of that time-honored protection.[38]

V

From the onset of Reconstruction until the end of World War I, the history of personal liberty performed like a compass moving through the Bermuda Triangle: it whirled and pointed every which way. Even though the words became more commonplace in American culture than ever before, they carried markedly different meanings for diverse segments of society. Some of these meanings were regressive, but others were way ahead of their time. In no other phase of our history did the phrase resound more, yet mean less. The best that we can do is note the predominant directions on that gyrating compass.

First and most obvious, passage of the Thirteenth Amendment in 1865 seemed (and in fact was) a stunning step forward for advocates of personal liberty. When Justice Samuel Miller delivered the Court's opinion in the *Slaughter-House Cases* (1873), he even incorporated the text of that amendment and praised "this grand yet simple declaration of the personal freedom of all the human race within the jurisdiction of this government."[39]

Second, and more important though much less obvious, passage of the Fourteenth Amendment in 1866 and ratification two years after that surely must have expanded the meaning of personal liberty even more. Senator Jacob M. Howard of Michigan, discussing the amendment in 1866, referred to "the personal rights guaranteed" by the first eight amendments in the Bill of Rights. More than a century later, in *Roe* v. *Wade*, the Supreme Court's controversial decision upholding a woman's right to have an abortion, Justice Potter Stewart concurred that "the right asserted by Jane Roe is embraced within the personal liberty protected by the Due Process Clause" of the Fourteenth Amendment. Justice Powell proposed a similar rationale.[40]

Although "liberty" is mentioned with some frequency in the justices' opinions concerning abortion, the text of the Fourteenth Amendment never mentions personal liberty. Nor does the Constitution itself. Nevertheless, Supreme Court decisions that developed in the wake of *Roe* v. *Wade* candidly built upon precedents that carried a greater weight of fairness and ethical concern for the pregnant female than of constitutional solidity. A 1977 decision, for example, written by Justice Brennan, absorbed much of the language of *Roe* v. *Wade*, acknowledged that "although 'the Constitution does not explicitly mention any right of privacy,' the Court has recognized that one aspect of the 'liberty' protected by the Due Process Clause of the Fourteenth Amendment is 'a right of personal privacy, or a guarantee of certain areas or zones of privacy.'"[41] The wonderfully elastic Fourteenth Amendment has come to be regarded by jurists as a major milestone in the history of a concept about which it is essentially mute.

A third trend pertinent in this period involved a far more tortured use of the Fourteenth Amendment to uphold a doctrine labeled "liberty to contract." Various pieces of protective, prolabor legislation from the states were declared unconstitutional because they deprived someone of the "personal liberty" of working — for instance, unusually long hours under unhealthy conditions. This was not only the essence of Justice Rufus Peckham's opinion for the Court in the notorious case of *Lochner* v. *New York* (1905),[42] but of Justice John Marshall Harlan in *Adair* v. *United States* (1908), a decision that upheld "yellow-dog contracts" (by invalidating a statute that protected labor union membership) on grounds that the law exceeded Congress's power to regulate interstate commerce and violated the freedom of contract guaranteed by the Fifth Amendment. Harlan's language and reasoning are so representative of the era that a lengthy extract seems warranted:

> It is not within the power of Congress to make it a criminal offense against the United States for a carrier engaged in interstate commerce, or an agent or officer thereof, to discharge an employé simply because of his membership in a labor organization; and the provision to that effect . . . concerning interstate carriers is an invasion of personal liberty, as well as of the right of property. . . . It was the defendant Adair's right — and that right inhered in his personal liberty, and was also a right of property. . . . Is this a fair, reasonable and appropriate exercise of the police power of the State, or is it an unreasonable, unnecessary and arbitrary interference with the right of the individual to his personal liberty or to enter into those contracts in relation to labor which may seem to him appropriate or necessary for the support of himself and his family?[43]

Justice Oliver Wendell Holmes dissented, just as he had in *Lochner;* but this time, given Harlan's emphatic yet (to Holmes) perverse use of "personal liberty," Holmes briefly articulated his understanding of that concept: namely, "the paramount individual rights, secured by the Fifth Amendment."[44] A year later Roscoe Pound reinforced Holmes's position with a resounding essay that put reverse spin on the history of our concept. "Personal liberty is always subject to restraint," wrote Pound, drawing upon a recent decision by the Court of Appeals of New York, "when its exercise affects the safety, health or moral and general welfare of the public, but subject to such restraint, an employer and employee may make and enforce such contract relating to labor as they may agree on."[45]

What should happen if personal liberty conflicted directly with interests of the state? The answer, in any given situation, depended upon ideology, circumstances, and whether or not the state's interest was "compelling." In 1907, for example, the Supreme Court decided (eight to one) that private individuals had "unlawfully exposed to public view, sold . . . and had in their possession for sale a bottle of beer, upon which, for purposes of advertisement, was printed and painted a representation of the flag of the United States." The defendants had pleaded not guilty, insisting that the Nebraska law under which they were prosecuted was null and void "as infringing their personal liberty" guaranteed by the Fourteenth Amendment. The state of Illinois had already held such a statute unconstitutional on several grounds, among them "infringing the personal liberty" guaranteed by the state and federal constitutions.[46]

In the High Court's opinion, however, the state's desire to cultivate feelings of patriotism constituted a legitimate basis for constraining personal liberty. Justice Harlan elucidated the Court's ban upon beer bottles that desecrated Old Glory:

> We cannot hold that any privilege of American citizenship or that any right of personal liberty is violated by a state enactment forbidding the flag to be used as an advertisement on a bottle of beer. The privileges of citizenship and the rights inhering in personal liberty are subject, in their enjoyment, to such reasonable restraints as may be required for the general good.[47]

Justice Harlan had not consistently taken an antilibertarian position, however. Writing one of the great dissents in Supreme Court history, he opposed the doctrine of "separate but equal" in *Plessy* v. *Ferguson*. That case involved the racial segregation of railroad cars by the state of Louisiana. Harlan opposed his brethren on the explicit basis of Blackstone's concern for freedom of movement. "The fundamental objection . . . to the statute," Harlan wrote, "is that it interferes with the personal freedom of citizens. 'Personal liberty,' it has been well said, 'consists in the power of locomotion, of changing situation, or removing one's person to whatsoever place one's own inclination may direct, without imprisonment or restraint, unless by due course of law.'" Straight from Blackstone's *Commentaries*. Six pages later Harlan concluded in his own words: "I am of opinion that the statute of Louisiana is inconsistent with the personal liberty of citizens, white and black, in the State, and hostile to both the spirit and letter of the Constitution of the United States."[48]

Few other voices were effectively raised on behalf of personal liberty during these years. One might hear the phrase mentioned in the hortatory urgings of Eugene V. Debs, or encounter it in the writings of men so diverse as Brooks Adams and Upton Sinclair.[49] One could even find it in the work of America's most influential legal theorist during the later nineteenth and early twentieth century, Thomas M. Cooley. His book *Constitutional Limitations* (1868) does mention "jury trials and other safeguards to personal liberty," and in *A Treatise on the Law of Torts* (1879) Cooley anticipates the language of Brandeis and Douglas. "*Personal immunity*," as defined by Cooley, meant that "the right of one's person may be said to be a right of complete immunity; the right to be let alone."[50]

Cooley's treatises lent themselves in various ways to conservative interpretations, however, which may help to explain his remarkably broad appeal at that time. Be that as it may, the messages of presidents like Benjamin Harrison, and the jurisprudence of justices like Stephen J. Field and Stanley Matthews, were likely to be sprinkled with references to personal liberty, yet equally likely to sustain the needs of corporate interests or of the state as against the rights of individuals.[51]

VI

From World War I until the mid–twentieth century our concept continued to be utilized in contradictory ways, though the range of possibilities narrowed, and there were fewer instances (as with Cooley,

Field, and Matthews) of libertarian language being put to conservative purposes. In retrospect, at least, motives as well as discourse seem less convoluted. Opponents of prohibition, for example, insisted that their personal liberty was being violated. Conservatives like Chief Justice Taft and David Jayne Hill declared candidly that excessive application or expansion of the "democratic principle" threatened the freedom of action (meaning dominance) and personal liberty of those best qualified to understand what the founders had intended in 1787.[52]

A symptomatic public lecture that Taft presented in 1922 resounded with familiar chords from Alexander Hamilton, Gouverneur Morris, and other Whigs most protective of private property 135 years before. "The Federal Constitution today," Taft intoned, "guards a man in the enjoyment of his personal liberty, his property and his pursuit of happiness, whether violated by the Federal or State Government." Over and over again, Taft sang the same refrains:

> Our Constitution has been called too individualistic. It rests on personal liberty and the right of property. In the last analysis, personal liberty includes the right of property as it includes the right of contract and the right of labor.
>
> To be useful, democracy and liberty must be regulated.
>
> The rights of personal liberty and of property as protected by the courts are not obstructive to any reasonable qualification of these rights in the interest of the community.[53]

Were these the last gasps of "personal liberty" as a shibboleth on behalf of the status quo and resistance to compassionate social progress? Not quite. In Governor Franklin D. Roosevelt's final message to the New York State Assembly (1932), and in Herbert Hoover's ideological manifesto, *The Challenge to Liberty* (1934), personal liberty remained nearly synonymous with unfettered economic opportunity for the enterprising individual.[54]

Even so, significant signs of change could be spotted from the mid-1920s onward — shifts that would herald new meanings for personal liberty from the mid-1950s until the present. The shift began, unremarkably, with increased *thoughtfulness* about civil liberties even when those in authority persisted in repressing civil liberties. In its landmark decision involving the case of *Gitlow* v. *New York* (1925), the Supreme Court declared that freedom of speech and of the press "are among the fundamental personal rights and 'liberties'" protected by the Due Process Clause of the Fourteenth Amendment.[55]

A number of additional cases that came before the Court during the period 1931–38 elicited appeals on behalf of personal liberty that urged greater concern for the rights of petition and assembly; expanded concern for speech and press; and, by 1938, the Court's opinion in *Missouri ex. rel. Gaines* v. *Canada,* written by Charles Evans Hughes, considered the right to attend a law school in the state of one's residence a personal liberty.[56]

Meanwhile, various state-based civil liberties committees emerged and began fund-raising as well as public consciousness-raising activities. In 1936, moreover, the American Academy of Political and Social Science invited several individuals, selected for their diverse backgrounds, to prepare essays explicitly devoted to the theme of personal liberty. Congressman John W. McCormack, then a representative from Massachusetts, chairman of the Special House Committee Investigating Nazi and Un-American Activities, and subsequently Speaker of the House (1962–71), provided a fairly pedestrian article that primarily defined personal liberty in terms of the Bill of Rights. I suspect that his response may have been representative of the American mainstream at that time.[57]

A different sort of contribution came from Roger N. Baldwin, who had served as director of the American Civil Liberties Union in New York City since 1920. Baldwin's response was more realistic, complex, and prescient. He too acknowledged the "personal liberties set forth in the Bill of Rights," but Baldwin insisted that they had been "adopted not by the founding fathers but by the pressure of the people themselves," and added that they "rest on two sets of guarantees — those protecting freedom of agitation, and those protecting defendants on trial." He recognized the complex implications of Roosevelt's New Deal reforms for traditional American perceptions of personal freedom, and called attention to these emerging tensions in his opening paragraph:

> "Personal liberty" at once arouses the concept of freedom from restraint in habits of living. Its most vivid recent application involved the attempted philosophy which justified violating the prohibition amendment. Its loudest immediate application concerns the rights of private property in the conflict between rugged individualism and state control. Less vocal but more in the American tradition are the genuine libertarians whose politi-

cal thinking, running back to the founding fathers and beyond, regards liberty as the priceless possession of free men to agitate, to alter governments, to remold economic systems.[58]

In recognizing that big government, regardless of which party controlled it, could pose a threat to personal liberty, Baldwin offered a cautionary note that has become more meaningful, rather than less, in the half century since.

The 1939–40 term of the U.S. Supreme Court marked the beginning of a new day in its preoccupation with issues involving one or another aspect of personal liberty. In that volume of *U.S. Reports* (no. 310), the index entry for "Constitutional Law, Fourteenth Amendment, Due Process Clause," includes eighteen cases — an unprecedented number. The volume for 1943 (no. 319) is the first to have a separate index subentry for "personal liberty" under "Constitutional Law."

Needless to say, this hardly meant that the apogee of personal liberty had been achieved. In 1943, after all, the Court decided *Hirabayashi* v. *United States*, and the following year *Korematsu* v. *United States*, two of the cases that sanctioned wartime internment for more than 110,000 Japanese-Americans living on the Pacific coast. It does seem noteworthy, however, that Edward J. Ennis, director of the Justice Department's Alien Enemy Control Unit, who fought valiantly on behalf of the Japanese-Americans, framed his queries for the Supreme Court in terms of "traditional standards of personal liberty" in the United States.[59] Perhaps one might say that the tragedy occurred, in part, because those standards were not "traditional" enough, or were not sufficiently ingrained to protect personal liberties when racism became virulent.

Willful large-scale violations of the rights of Japanese-Americans constituted yet another unattractive example of what can happen when the quest for security (or else the relentless apprehension of insecurity) causes Americans to violate their vaunted traditions of liberty. A variation on that theme, sparked by hysterical anxiety over communism, led to the unattractive episode in our political culture that is encapsulated in a single word: McCarthyism. The damage done to personal liberty during that fevered phase — ranging from reputation to employment — has now been thoroughly documented.[60]

Even when such a bizarre melodrama was being played out, other episodes led to steady yet unspectacular victories for an expansion of the meaning of personal liberty in America. Many of these victories involved First Amendment freedoms — more particularly, the issue of school prayer[61] — and caused those freedoms to be called, during the 1940s and 1950s, "preferred freedoms," which meant that in case of conflict they should enjoy a higher status than subsequent amendments in the Bill of Rights.[62]

There are diverse ways to discern and particularize the great transformation that personal liberty underwent between the early 1940s and the 1970s in the United States. One way would utilize the constitutional treatment of obscene language and freedom of expression. In the case of *Chaplinsky* v. *New Hampshire* (1942), Justice Frank Murphy, one of the Supreme Court's most liberal members, upheld Chaplinsky's conviction for uttering "fighting words" to a policeman. Murphy developed his definitional test in this passage:

> There are certain well-defined and narrowly limited classes of speech, the prevention and punishment of which have never been thought to raise any Constitutional problem. These include the lewd and obscene, the profane, the libelous, and the insulting or "fighting" words — those which by their very utterance inflict injury or tend to incite an immediate breach of the peace.[63]

In 1971 the case of *Cohen* v. *California* came before the Supreme Court. It concerned the prosecution of a man who protested the Vietnam war at a Los Angeles courthouse by wearing a jacket with the words "Fuck the Draft" emblazoned across the back. This time Justice John Marshall Harlan, one of the most conservative members of the Court, wrote its decision:

> While the particular four-letter word being litigated here is perhaps more distasteful than most others of its genre, it is nevertheless often true that one man's vulgarity is another's lyric. Indeed, we think it is largely because governmental officials cannot make principled distinctions in this area that the Constitution leaves matters of taste and style so largely to the individual.[64]

American decorum may have deteriorated; but perhaps it can be said that the notion of personal liberty expanded, at the very least, and perhaps even progressed between 1942 and 1971.[65]

VII

During the past few decades, in my view, more genuinely new dimensions have been added to the notion of personal liberty than at any other time in our entire history. The concept has achieved levels of complexity, richness, and controversy previously unimagined. In part these developments resulted from technological revolutions that had implications ranging from silent governmental surveillance of the individual to matters involving sexual intimacy and means of dealing with unwanted consequences of such intimacy. Above all, however, these developments are linked to the concept of a right to privacy, a right perceived as extraconstitutional when first proposed by Louis D. Brandeis and Samuel D. Warren in 1890, yet one that gradually has become (or perhaps is becoming) "constitutionalized" since 1965.

Although the cultural and legal history of a "right to privacy" would require a whole separate volume,[66] we can at least look at some of the ways in which it has made the concept of personal liberty more meaningful (and more palpable) than ever before. The explication by Brandeis and Warren was stimulated by the increasing intrusiveness of low-level journalism upon American life in general and its impact upon personal reputation in particular—what the two lawyers designated with an ungainly yet memorable phrase as the "newspaperization" of private life. The authors believed that government was already constrained to respect an individual's right to privacy; they urged that comparable constraints be placed upon newspapers and similar sources of gossip-mongering. But they contended that a right to privacy was implicit in the common law, "as a part of the more general right to the immunity of the person—the right to one's personality." The right to privacy, therefore, was a torts concept rather than a constitutional right.[67]

In 1928, twelve years after he had been named to the U.S. Supreme Court, a case arose that caused Brandeis to feel less sanguine about the normatively benign role of government. The issue involved wiretapping and the government's use of evidence obtained illegally. Brandeis's brethren approved; but his trenchant dissent would be an exceedingly important harbinger of new directions in American constitutionalism more than a generation later. Brandeis used a lengthy extract from an 1886 case in order to review the historical background of the Fourth and Fifth Amendments, more particularly government invasion of the sanctities of one's home and the private aspects of one's life. What had become unacceptable in the Anglo-American tradition was "the invasion of [a person's] indefeasible right of personal security, personal liberty and private property, where that right has never been forfeited by his conviction of some public offence." Four pages later Brandeis boldly introduced a phrase that has acquired considerable momentum in our own time — a phrase that connects, as no other could, the right to privacy with personal liberty:

> The makers of our Constitution . . . conferred, as against the Government, the right to be let alone — the most comprehensive of rights and the right most valued by civilized men. To protect that right, every unjustifiable intrusion by the Government upon the privacy of the individual, whatever the means employed, must be deemed a violation of the Fourth Amendment.[68]

Despite that eloquent dissent, the Supreme Court remained very muddled on this matter right through the 1950s, and spoke with varied voices concerning the question of when illegally obtained evidence was admissible: not when brutality, physical assault or coercion had been used, apparently, yet acceptable when trespass, burglary, or the planting of microphones by police had been authorized. What rationale legitimized these distinctions is not clear; but the fact remains that until the decision in *Mapp* v. *Ohio* (1961), the Fourth Amendment did not apply to the states. Writing the Court's opinion in that case, Justice Tom C. Clark acknowledged the existence of "constitutional documentation of the right of privacy free from unreasonable state intrusion."[69]

In 1960, meanwhile, quite a different aspect of personal liberty and the right to privacy received the Court's imprimatur. The question that arose involved whether or not compulsory disclosure of membership lists of local branches of the National Association for the Advancement of Colored People would interfere with the freedom of association of members. Justice Potter Stewart defined the issue in this manner: had the cities, as instrumentalities of the state, demonstrated so cogent a public interest in obtaining and making public membership lists as to justify the substantial abridgment of associational freedom? Stewart responded with caution and prudence. "Where there is a significant encroachment upon personal liberty," he wrote, "the State may prevail only upon showing a subordinating interest which is compelling."[70]

Justice William O. Douglas helped to prepare the way for these decisions during the 1950s by building upon the two concepts that Louis D. Brandeis had introduced in 1890 and 1928. A case came before the High Court in 1952 because the Washington, D.C., transit system decided to enhance its revenues by installing continuous radio broadcasting on its buses. Although the Court approved, Douglas dissented because he objected to any form of coerced listening. His language is stirring, but also important because it anticipated major developments in constitutional doctrine that took place during the 1960s and 1970s. Douglas grounded his argument as much in natural right, or in constitutional implications, as he did in the Constitution itself:

> Liberty in the constitutional sense must mean more than freedom from unlawful government restraint; it must include privacy as well, if it is to be a repository of freedom. The right to be let alone is indeed the beginning of all freedom. . . . The right of privacy should include the right to pick and choose from competing entertainments, competing propaganda, competing political philosophies. If people are let alone in those choices, the right of privacy will pay dividends in character and integrity.[71]

Less than six years later Douglas expanded upon this theme in reaching a much wider lay audience. The longest section in a published collection of lectures first given at Franklin and Marshall College was entitled "The Right to Be Let Alone"; and the first installment of that section Douglas called "The Right of Privacy." Having linked economic opportunity with personal freedom in the 1940s, he moved during the 1950s toward positions that some others would come to share in the next decade — yet remain controversial among jurists and scholars to this day. Referring to personal liberty and privacy as "natural rights," he insisted in 1958 that some of these rights had been "written explicitly into the Constitution. Others are to be implied. The penumbra of the Bill of Rights reflects human rights which, though not explicit, are implied from the very nature of man as a child of God."[72]

Quite early in his career on the Court, Douglas staunchly opposed intervention by the state in the intimate relationships or reproductive rights of an individual. In 1942, for example, he wrote the High Court's opinion reversing a judgment by the Supreme Court of Oklahoma that the state could legally sterilize a man who was a habitual criminal.

In 1961, when the U.S. Supreme Court refused to overturn Connecticut's law prohibiting the sale of contraceptives, Douglas supplied a resounding dissent.[73]

Thereafter others on the Court became willing to follow the path that Douglas had pioneered for years. The decision in 1965 to overturn Connecticut's ban on contraceptives is too familiar to require extended commentary here. The point more pertinent to this essay is that Justices Goldberg and White quoted Potter Stewart's assertion in *Bates* v. *Little Rock* (1960): "Where there is a significant encroachment upon personal liberty, the State may prevail only upon showing a subordinating interest which is compelling." White characterized reproductive decisions as being within the "sensitive areas of liberty" protected by the Court; and Goldberg proscribed governmental invasion of marital privacy.[74]

Seven years later Justice William Brennan wrote the court's opinion that extended the implications of *Griswold* to unmarried persons. "If the right to privacy means anything," he declared, "it is the right of the *individual*, married or single, to be free from unwarranted governmental intrusion into matters so fundamentally affecting a person as the decision whether to bear or beget a child."[75] In a major expansion of the widely questioned basis for the 1965 decision, the Supreme Court now recognized that a right to privacy unfolded from the right to personal liberty in a general sense, rather than emerging from murky penumbras created by various articles in the Bill of Rights.

In retrospect it seems almost inevitable that Justice Blackmun's decision in *Roe* v. *Wade* would derive a woman's right to terminate her pregnancy from "the concept of personal 'liberty' embodied" in the Due Process Clause of the Fourteenth Amendment. Justice Stewart's concurrence used language that was technically more correct in acknowledging the act of judicial interpretation: "The right asserted by Jane Roe is embraced within the personal liberty protected" by the Due Process Clause.[76]

VIII

There is considerably more to the story of personal liberty and the right to privacy — a relationship that has become particularly interesting and complex during the past quarter century. Since 1965 the Supreme Court has tended to protect "personal privacy" on the grounds that it is inherent in the term "liberty." Lest the preceding section convey an impression of emerging consensus and steady progress, however, it seems prudent to conclude by noting some patterns of inconsistency.

Two cases that came to the High Court from Georgia are indicative of ups and downs if not outright inconsistency. In 1969 the Court ruled that persons may possess and view obscene films in the privacy of their homes. As Justice Thurgood Marshall explained on behalf of the majority, "mere categorization of these films as 'obscene' is insufficient justification for such a drastic invasion of personal liberties guaranteed by the First and Fourteenth Amendments." In 1986, however, the Court ruled (by a sharply contested vote of five to four) that a Georgia law prohibiting sodomy could stand. Twenty-three other states also have such laws. As the *New York Times* summarized the situation: "The Constitution does not protect homosexual relations between consenting adults, even in the privacy of their own homes."[77]

Why does the concept of a right to privacy, protected by the Fourteenth Amendment, justify the sale of contraceptives (even to unmarried minors), a woman's decision to have an abortion, and the privilege of watching any sort of film in one's home, but not homosexual acts performed by consenting adults in private? It may be quite some time before the inconsistency is clarified or rectified. Much will depend upon whether President Reagan has the opportunity to name additional justices to the Supreme Court before his term ends.

Mr. Reagan seems to have a low regard for the right of privacy. In September, 1986, he directed the heads of federal agencies to establish programs designed to test for drug abuse (through urinalysis) among a broad range of government employees. Three days after the President's mandate appeared, a judge at the Federal District Court in Newark, New Jersey, declared it an unconstitutional invasion of privacy. By the end of 1986, lawsuits had successfully stopped thirteen out of seventeen programs for random drug testing on the grounds that such tests violate the Fourth Amendment protection against unreasonable search and seizure.[78] Where certain sorts of issues are concerned, the Reagan administration appears to follow the policy that a person is guilty until proven innocent.

Although it is possible, and even historically sensible, to say that notions of personal liberty have come a long way in American thought and culture, a sampling of statements made by prominent opinion-shapers in 1986–87 suggests that resistance to change remains strong. The mainstream apparently prefers moderate balancing. Justice Hugo Black's belief in absolute governmental guarantees of those freedoms protected by the Constitution is not currently fashionable. On the eve of Liberty Weekend in 1986, the widely respected James Reston had this to say:

> In the civil life of the nation, personal liberty has a lovely sound but often means license to break the law, traffic in drugs, abandon families and put personal or special interests ahead of the general good. . . . The modern nation-state, operating for the first time in a complicated world economy, has to find practical ways of reconciling personal liberty with the general welfare if it is to compete successfully with other industrial nations.[79]

Quite frankly, it never occurred to me — nor did it occur to the framers — that personal rights protected by the U.S. Constitution would ever have to be subordinated to the exigencies of international economic competition. Adam Smith does not yet rank above John Milton, Roger Williams, Thomas Jefferson, Frederick Douglass, or Louis D. Brandeis in my pantheon of heroes or my hierarchy of values.

In 1984 the United States Catholic Bishops' Ad Hoc Committee on Catholic Social Teaching and the U.S. Economy produced a pastoral letter that urged the government to adopt more compassionate economic policies in order to achieve a "just economic order," particularly for the "poor and deprived members of the human community." That might require some governmental intervention in the marketplace; but, once again, it seems fair to point out that Adam Smith has been dead since 1790.[80]

Not, however, for the Lay Commission on Catholic Social Teaching and the U.S. Economy. That conservative group wrote a rebuttal to the bishops that tendentiously condemned "radical individualism." It also called for necessary counterweights to personal liberty:

> Every human society must strike a proper balance between individual liberty and common action. The American experiment has entailed a keen struggle to find that balance. On the one side is the unique commitment of our people to personal liberty, as enshrined in and animating the fed-

eral Constitution. On the other is the central presupposition of that historical document: that our vigorous familial and communal life continue healthy and strong, a common unity. Strong families and strong communities teach those personal virtues without which the Constitution cannot be preserved, and provide care for those who are in need of help and guidance.[81]

If the concept of personal liberty has not only grown but changed over time, there is little wisdom in the assumption that it should change no more. What is curious about the lay commission's letter, however, is that it represents a reactionary return to the Calvinist value system of Massachusetts Bay. There is much to admire in that value system; but we must not lose sight of the fact that the socio-economic circumstances of a seventeenth-century colony are several hundred light years removed from our own.

We should also keep in mind that the meaning of personal liberty has repeatedly been altered over time, in part because the concept is not explicitly mentioned in the U.S. Constitution. It is not frozen into a singular form by virtue of inclusion in a sacred text. Insofar as it has variously meant liberty of conscience, opposition to chattel slavery, freedom from physical restraint, freedom of political association, freedom from surveillance where no threat to the state is involved, and a right to privacy that includes control over one's body, it has drawn upon both of the great traditions of liberty: negative as well as positive freedom, "freedom from" and "freedom to."

As Justices Brandeis and Douglas so eloquently explained, the concept of personal liberty is considerably older than our Constitution.[82] The latter *began* to catch up with the former in 1789, with passage of the Bill of Rights. It gained additional ground in 1866, with passage of the Fourteenth Amendment. It achieved a significant degree of reconceptualization between 1928 and 1965; and since then the notion of a constitutional right to privacy has infused personal liberty with palpable new meaning.

In historical terms, I cannot conceive of a more significant phenomenon in our culture than the spasmodic adjustment of American constitutionalism to the process whereby we discover new imperatives in those two simple words, "personal liberty." In contemporary terms, I cannot imagine a more significant social and political agenda than the ongoing clarification of what we mean by personal liberty in response to our growing concern for human happiness, dignity and autonomy.

NOTES

1. See Kammen, *Spheres of Liberty: Changing Perceptions of Liberty in American Culture* (Madison: University of Wisconsin Press, 1986).

2. Hughes, "Liberty and Law," *Report of the 48th Annual Meeting of the American Bar Association* (Baltimore, 1925), 187; Roosevelt on March 9, 1937, in Samuel I. Rosenman, comp., *The Public Papers and Addresses of Franklin D. Roosevelt* (New York: Random House, 1938), 6:132; *New York Times*, 16 June 1965, 8. See also William J. Brennan, Jr., "Landmarks of Legal Liberty," in Bernard Schwartz, ed., *The Fourteenth Amendment: Centennial Volume* (New York: New York University Press, 1970), 2.

3. See Peter Clecak, *America's Quest for the Ideal Self: Dissent and Fulfillment in the 60s and 70s* (New York: Oxford University Press, 1983), 12; Laurence H. Tribe, *God Save This Honorable Court: How the Choice of Supreme Court Justices Shapes Our History* (New York: Random House, 1985), 11–12, 35; Richard Kluger, *Simple Justice: The History of* Brown v. Board of Education *and Black America's Struggle for Equality* (New York: Knopf, 1975), 36, 241. On pp. 88 and 118 Kluger at least offers a brief definition: "the right of the citizen to free association in his private dealings."

4. "The Court's Right Turn," *Nation*, June 28, 1986, 1. See also Eleanor Blau, "Personal Freedoms: Topic of Liberty Weekend Sessions," *New York Times*, 22 June 1986, p. A26.

5. See George Bancroft to Mrs. J. C. B. Davis, 3 October 1870, in Mark De Wolfe Howe, *The Life and Letters of George Bancroft* (New York: Scribner's, 1908), 2:243; Charles Francis Adams, "The Progress of Liberty," an address given at Taunton, Mass., on 4 July 1876, published as an "Extra" pamphlet by the *New-York Tribune*, 32–33.

6. See the Anti-Federalist who wrote as "Brutus" (29 November 1787), and Thomas Jefferson to James Madison, 15 March 1789, both in Michael Kammen, ed., *The Origins of the American Constitution: A Documentary History* (New York: Penguin Books, 1986), 327, 377.

7. Jacob E. Cooke, ed., *The Federalist* (Middletown, Conn.: Wesleyan University Press, 1961), 57, 61.

8. Both James Otis (1764) and Martin Howard (1765) distinguished between political and personal rights ("life, liberty, and estate"). Howard contended that personal rights were secured by the common law tradition. Similarly, the *Encyclopaedia Britannica* (first published 1778–83), differentiated, in the entry for "Liberty," between political and personal liberty. Under "personal immunities" it included the rights of personal security, personal liberty, and private property. See Bernard Bailyn, ed., *Pamphlets of the American Revolution, 1750–1776* (Cambridge, Mass.: Harvard University Press, 1965), 1:535, 538; Gaetano Salvemini, "The Concepts of Democracy and Liberty in the Eighteenth Century," in Conyers Read, ed., *The Constitution Reconsidered*, 2nd ed. (New York: Harper & Row, 1968), 113.

9. See, e.g., A. Lawrence Lowell, *Essays on Government* (Boston: Houghton, Mifflin, 1889), 60, 62. See also Edward S. Corwin to A. A. Hamblen, Jan. 9, 1940, Corwin Papers, Seeley G. Mudd Library, Princeton University: "Have you ever given con-

sideration to the idea that the term 'liberty' as used in legal philosophy has two different meanings; 1. civil liberty which is that liberty that we enjoy in consequence of the
restraints which the ordinary law imposes upon our neighbors; 2. constitutional liberty
or the liberty which comes when one is entitled to appeal against the restrictions which
government and the ordinary law imposes upon our own actions. I think a little reflection will convince you that the former is much the more important, and that the latter
—which we have so much emphasized in this country—while important, is distinctly
of less importance than civil liberty."

10. 16 *Wallace* 115 (1873).

11. See Edward S. Corwin, *Liberty against Government: The Rise, Flowering
and Decline of a Famous Juridical Concept* (Baton Rouge: Louisiana State University
Press, 1948), 140; Charles E. Shattuck, "The True Meaning of the Term 'Liberty' in
Those Clauses in the Federal and State Constitutions Which Protect 'Life, Liberty, and
Property,'" *Harvard Law Review* 4 (March, 1891): 369, 373–77.

12. Robert G. McCloskey, ed., *The Works of James Wilson* (Cambridge, Mass.:
Harvard University Press, 1967), 2:588–89; Timothy Dwight in Charles S. Hyneman
and Donald S. Lutz, eds., *American Political Writing during the Founding Era, 1760–
1805* (Indianapolis: Liberty Press, 1983), 2:888–89.

13. Shattuck, "True Meaning," 376; Charles H. McIlwain, *Constitutionalism: Ancient and Modern* (Ithaca, N.Y.: Cornell University Press, 1947), 127.

14. H. T. Dickinson, *Liberty and Property: Political Ideology in Eighteenth-
Century Britain* (New York: Holmes and Meier, 1977), 68; A. J. Carlyle, *Political Liberty: A History of the Conception in the Middle Ages and Modern Times* (Oxford: Oxford University Press, 1941), chap. 1.

15. A. S. P. Woodhouse, ed., *Puritanism and Liberty: Being the Army Debates
(1647–9)* . . . (Chicago: University of Chicago Press, 1951), 59–60, 65–67, 80.

16. Locke, *Two Tracts on Government*, ed. Philip Abrams (Cambridge: Cambridge University Press, 1967), 129, 142.

17. Edmund S. Morgan, *The Puritan Dilemma: The Story of John Winthrop* (Boston: Little, Brown, 1958), 10; Oscar and Mary Handlin, *The Dimensions of Liberty*
(Cambridge, Mass.: Harvard University Press, 1961), 58, 71.

18. Lengthy extracts from Wise and Williams will be found in Edmund S. Morgan, ed., *Puritan Political Ideas, 1558–1794* (Indianapolis: Bobbs-Merrill, 1965), 257,
269, 285–87.

19. See anon., "Four Letters on Interesting Subjects" (Philadelphia, 1776) in Hyneman and Lutz, eds., *American Political Writing during the Founding Era*, 1:381; Levi
Hart, *Liberty Described and Recommended; in a sermon, preached to the Corpora-
tion of Freemen in Farmington . . . Sept. 20, 1774* (Hartford: Ebenezer Watson, 1775),
14, 22; Melvin B. Endy, Jr., "Just War, Holy War, and Millennialism in Revolutionary
America," *William and Mary Quarterly* 42 (January, 1985): 12.

20. Alexis de Tocqueville, *Democracy in America*, ed. J. P. Mayer (Garden City,
N.Y.: Anchor Books, 1969), 293. Cf. William G. McLoughlin, "The Role of Religion
in the Revolution: Liberty of Conscience and Cultural Cohesion in the New Nation,"
in Stephen G. Kurtz and James H. Hutson, eds., *Essays on the American Revolution*
(Chapel Hill: University of North Carolina Press, 1973), 197–255.

21. See *Pennsylvania Journal and Weekly Advertiser*, February 23, 1758, quoted
in Lawrence Leder, *Liberty and Authority: Early American Political Ideology, 1689–
1763* (Chicago: Quadrangle Books, 1968), 121; and Benjamin F. Wright, *Consensus and
Continuity, 1776–1787* (New York: Norton, 1967), 13.

22. See Locke, *Two Treatises of Government*, ed. Peter Laslett (Cambridge: Cambridge University Press, 1960), chap. 4, "Of Slavery," 301–3.

23. Montesquieu, *The Spirit of Laws* [sic], ed. David Wallace Carrithers (Berkeley: University of California Press, 1977), 215–17. For the French philosopher Jean Louis De Lolme, see Salvemini, "The Concepts of Democracy and Liberty," 113.

24. Max Farrand, ed., *The Records of the Federal Convention of 1787*, 2nd ed. (New Haven, Conn.: Yale University Press, 1937), 1:512 (Morris spoke on July 2). See also William Grayson's remarks in the Confederation Congress on 27 September 1787, in Merrill Jensen, ed., *The Documentary History of the Ratification of the Constitution* (Madison: State Historical Society of Wisconsin, 1976), 1:331.

25. See McCloskey, *Works of James Wilson*, 2:648–49; Brennan, "Landmarks of Legal Liberty," 8.

26. Cooke, *The Federalist*, 57.

27. Quoted in Catherine Drinker Bowen, *Miracle at Philadelphia: The Story of the Constitutional Convention, May to September 1787* (Boston: Little, Brown, 1966), 71.

28. See Robert C. Palmer, *Liberties as Constitutional Provisions, 1776–1791* (Williamsburg, Va.: Institute of Bill of Rights Law, George Wythe School of Law, 1987), esp. n. 255.

29. James A. Haw, ed., "Samuel Chase's 'Objections to the Federal Government,'" *Maryland Historical Magazine* 76 (September, 1981): 277.

30. Jefferson to Washington, [4 December] 1788, in Julian P. Boyd, ed., *The Papers of Thomas Jefferson* (Princeton, N.J.: Princeton University Press, 1958), 14:332; Max Farrand, *The Framing of the Constitution of the United States* (New Haven, Conn.: Yale University Press, 1913), 163.

31. Wilson, "Lectures on Law" (1790), in McCloskey, *Works of James Wilson*, 2:648.

32. Quoted in Sean Wilentz, *Chants Democratic: New York City & the Rise of the American Working Class, 1788–1850* (New York: Oxford University Press, 1984), 44.

33. For Justice Joseph Story in 1829, e.g., see Corwin, *Liberty Against Government*, 67. For a highly representative decision made by the Supreme Court of Vermont in 1855, see Charles Warren, "The New 'Liberty' under the Fourteenth Amendment," *Harvard Law Review* 39 (February, 1926): 443–44.

34. See James D. Richardson, comp., *A Compilation of the Messages and Papers of the Presidents, 1789–1897* (Washington, D.C.: U.S. Congress, 1896–99), 2:303; 4:7, 336.

35. Ramsay, "Poverty," [Charleston, S.C.] *City Gazette and Daily Advertiser*, 8 December 1789, in Hyneman and Lutz, eds., *American Political Writing*, 2:723.

36. See Thomas D. Morris, *Free Men All: The Personal Liberty Laws of the North, 1780–1861* (Baltimore: Johns Hopkins University Press, 1974).

37. Noah Porter, *Civil Liberty: A Sermon Preached in Farmington, Connecticut, July 13, 1856* (New York: Pudney & Russell Printers, 1856), 6; James Barnett, *Personal Liberty for All Men* (Albany, N.Y.: Weed, Parsons, Printers, 1860).

38. See Edward Ingersoll, *Personal Liberty and Martial Law: A Review of Some Pamphlets of the Day* (Philadelphia: n.p., 1862); Carl B. Swisher, *Stephen J. Field: Craftsman of the Law* (Washington, D.C.: Brookings Institution, 1930), 136.

39. See Stanley I. Kutler, ed., *The Supreme Court and the Constitution: Readings in American Constitutional History*, 2nd ed. (New York: Norton, 1977), 227. See also Miller's use of "personal rights" in *Davidson* v. *New Orleans*, 96 U.S. 97 (1878), at 101–2.

40. Richard C. Cortner, *The Supreme Court and the Second Bill of Rights: The Fourteenth Amendment and the Nationalization of Civil Liberties* (Madison: University of Wisconsin Press, 1981), 5; *Roe* v. *Wade*, 410 U.S. 113–78 (1973), esp. 129, 153, 170.

41. *Carey* v. *Population Services International*, 431 U.S. 678 (1977), at 684; Judith A. Baer, *Equality under the Constitution: Reclaiming the Fourteenth Amendment* (Ithaca, N.Y.: Cornell University Press, 1983), 234. See also Charles Evans Hughes, *The Supreme Court of the United States: Its Foundation, Methods and Achievements* (New York: Columbia University Press, 1928), 166, where he included freedom of speech and of the press "among the fundamental personal rights and liberties" protected by the Due Process Clause of the Fourteenth Amendment.

42. For Peckham's use of personal liberty in this opinion, see Kutler, *Supreme Court*, 283–84.

43. *Adair* v. *United States*, 208 U.S. 161 (1908), at 161, 172, 174. For a very similar case, in which Justice Mahlon Pitney's opinion for the Court also invoked personal liberty serveral times, see *Coppage* v. *State of Kansas*, 236 U.S. 1 (1919), esp. at 2.

44. *Adair* v. *United States*, 208 U.S. 191.

45. Pound, "Liberty of Contract," *Yale Law Journal* 18 (May, 1909): 481. The opinion cited by Pound is *People* v. *Marcus*, 85 N.Y. 255 (1906).

46. *Halter* v. *Nebraska*, 205 U.S. 34 (1907), at 38–40.

47. Ibid., 42.

48. *Plessy* v. *Ferguson*, 163 U.S. 537 (1896), at 557 and 563. Harlan was not alone among his contemporaries in remembering Blackstone. Four years later Chief Justice Melville Fuller wrote: "Undoubtedly the right of locomotion, the right to remove from one place to another, according to inclination is an attribute of personal liberty" (*Williams* v. *Fears*, 179 U.S. 270 [1900] at 274). In a general revenue act, Georgia had passed a tax upon numerous occupations, including that of "emigrant agent," meaning a person engaged in hiring laborers to be employed beyond the limits of the state. Fuller's opinion asserted that personal liberty (as locomotion) was protected by the Fourteenth Amendment.

49. See Nick Salvatore, *Eugene V. Debs: Citizen and Socialist* (Urbana: University of Illinois Press, 1982), 153–54, 174–75, 191–92; Warren I. Susman, *Culture as History: The Transformation of American Society in the Twentieth Century* (New York: Pantheon, 1984), 46; Michael Kammen, *A Machine That Would Go of Itself: The Constitution in American Culture* (New York: Knopf, 1986), xvi.

50. See Corwin, *Liberty Against Government*, 117; Cooley, *A Treatise on the Law of Torts* (Chicago: Callaghan & Co., 1879), 29.

51. Harrison, Third Annual Message to Congress, 9 December 1891, in Richardson, comp., *Messages and Papers of the Presidents*, 9:197; Swisher, *Stephen J. Field*, 264; Matthews's opinion in *Hurtado* v. *California*, 110 U.S. 516 (1884), at 529, 530, 537.

52. For Hill, see "A Defense of the Constitution," *North American Review* 205 (March, 1917): 389–91, 395–96. For Charles Evans Hughes ("democracy has its own capacity for tyranny"), see "Liberty and Law" (1925), 187. See also George Bryan Logan, Jr., *Liberty in the Modern World* (Chapel Hill: University of North Carolina Press, 1928), 48, 67. Logan saw no inherent conflict between personal liberty and social control, and he urged that personal liberties be protected against the intolerance of popular government.

53. Taft, *Liberty under Law: An Interpretation of the Principles of Our Con-*

stitutional Government (New Haven, Conn.: Yale University Press, 1922), 14, 25–26, 40, 51.

54. Rosenman, *Public Papers and Addresses of Roosevelt*, 1:112; Hoover, *The Challenge to Liberty* (New York: Scribner's, 1934), 130, 163. Rowland Berthoff, "Peasants and Artisans, Puritans and Republicans: Personal Liberty and Communal Equality in American History," *Journal of American History* 69 (Dec. 1982), 582, 588, 594, 596, and 598, contends that achieving a balance between personal liberty and communal equality has been at the very core of the "American dream." Berthoff conflates personal liberty, however, with equal economic opportunity (esp. at 588). I insist that personal liberty has meant considerably more in American culture than merely bourgeois individualism.

55. *Gitlow v. New York*, 268 U.S. 652 (1925), at 666.

56. Cortner, *Supreme Court and the Second Bill of Rights*, 80, 81, 84, 94, 96–97; Herbert Wechsler, *Principles, Politics, and Fundamental Law: Selected Essays* (Cambridge, Mass.: Harvard University Press, 1961), 88; Kluger, *Simple Justice*, 213.

57. Harold Rotzel (executive secretary of the Civil Liberties Committee of Massachusetts) to Arthur M. Schlesinger, 23 October 1929, Schlesinger Papers, box 5, Harvard University Archives, Pusey Library, Cambridge, Mass.; John W. McCormack, "Personal Liberty," *Annals of the American Academy of Political and Social Science* 185 (May, 1936): 154–61.

58. Roger N. Baldwin, ibid., 162–69.

59. Peter Irons, *Justice at War* (New York: Oxford University Press, 1983), 183, 190. For a most ironic (and truly droll) aspect of Gordon K. Hirabayashi's quest for personal liberty, see 251.

60. See Ellen W. Schrecker, *No Ivory Tower: McCarthyism and the Universities* (New York: Oxford University Press, 1986).

61. See Vashti Cromwell McCollum, *One Woman's Fight* (Boston: Beacon Press, 1952), esp. 119.

62. It may be a minor irony of American constitutionalism that the best, most succinct history of the "preferred freedom doctrine" appears in a critical opinion by Felix Frankfurter in 1949 for the case of *Kovacs v. Cooper*, 336 U.S. 77, at 89–97.

63. *Chaplinsky v. New Hampshire*, 315 U.S. 568 (1942), at 571–72.

64. *Cohen v. California*, 403 U.S. 15 (1971), at 25.

65. For a thoughtful overview and case study, see Donald Alexander Downs, *Nazis in Skokie: Freedom, Community, and the First Amendment* (Notre Dame, Ind.: University of Notre Dame Press, 1985). See also Justice Rutledge concurring in the case of *In re Oliver*, 333 U.S. 257 (1948), at 280.

66. See a useful anthology developed for the classroom: P. Allan Dionisopoulos and Craig R. Ducat, eds., *The Right to Privacy: Essays and Cases* (St. Paul, Minn.: West Publishing Co., 1976).

67. Warren and Brandeis, "The Right to Privacy," *Harvard Law Review*, 4 (December, 1980): 207; Dorothy J. Glancy, "The Invention of the Right to Privacy," *Arizona Law Review* 21 (1979): 1–39.

68. *Olmstead v. United States*, 277 U.S. 438 (1928), at 474, 478. See also Brandeis concurring in *St. Josephs Stock Yards Co. v. U.S.* 298 U.S. 77 (1936).

69. Cortner, *The Supreme Court and the Second Bill of Rights*, 169–71, 185–86.

70. *Bates v. Little Rock*, 361 U.S. 516 (1960), at 524. See also *McLaughlin v. Florida*, 379 U.S. 184 (1964).

71. *Public Utilities Commission of the District of Columbia* v. *Pollak*, 343 U.S. 451 (1952), at 467–69. See also Dorothy J. Glancy, "Getting Government Off the Backs of People: The Right of Privacy and Freedom of Expression in the Opinions of Justice William O. Douglas," *Santa Clara Law Review*, 21 (1981): 1047–67.

72. Douglas, *The Right of the People* (Garden City, N.Y.: Doubleday, 1958), esp. 85–94, the quotation at 89; James F. Simon, *Independent Journey: The Life of William O. Douglas* (New York: Penguin Books, 1981), 251.

73. *Skinner* v. *Oklahoma*, 316 U.S. 535 (1942); *Poe* v. *Ullman*, 367 U.S. 497 (1961), at 517.

74. *Griswold* v. *Connecticut*, 381 U.S. 479 (1965), at 496–97, 503–4.

75. *Eisenstadt, Sheriff,* v. *Baird,* 405 U.S. 438 (1972), at 453.

76. *Roe* v. *Wade,* 410 U.S. 113 (1973), at 129, 152–53, 170. For a complex case involving a woman facing criminal charges concerning her allegedly irresponsible conduct during pregnancy, see *New York Times,* 9 October 1986, p. A22. The woman's child died (as a result of her behavior) soon after birth. The director of the ACLU reproductive freedom project, which is serving as the woman's co-counsel, has insisted that "a woman's right to privacy means the state is restricted from having any interest in her pregnancy."

77. *Stanley* v. *Georgia,* 394 U.S. 557 (1969), at 565; *Bowers* v. *Hardwick,* 106 S. Ct. 2841 (1986), reported in *New York Times,* 1 July 1986, 1.

78. See *New York Times,* 19 September 1986, 1; 13 November 1986, p. D27; and 11 December 1986, 1. For a citizen's damage suit involving privacy (illegal wiretapping and harassment) brought against federal agents by black and Vietnam peace activists, pending since 1976 and still being fought by the Justice Department, see *New York Times,* 28 September 1986, 35.

79. Reston, "Liberty and Authority," *New York Times,* 29 June 1986, p. E23.

80. "First Draft — Bishops' Pastoral: Catholic Social Teaching and the U.S. Economy," *Origins: N.C. Documentary Service* 14 (22/23): 337–38.

81. *Toward the Future: Catholic Social Thought and the U.S. Economy: A Lay Letter* (New York: American Catholic Committee, 1984), xi–xii.

82. The comparative history of personal liberty lies beyond the scope of this essay. For leads in the direction of such comparisons, however, I would suggest the following: Edward Muir, *Civic Ritual in Renaissance Venice* (Princeton, N.J.: Princeton University Press, 1981), 17; Frederic May Holland, *Liberty in the Nineteenth Century* (New York: Putnam's, 1899), 159–63, 202–6, 210–32; *Federal Constitution of Malaysia* (Kuala Lumpur, 1986), 3–4 ("Liberty of the Person"); The Constitution of India, Part III ("Fundamental Rights"), article 21, in Amos J. Peaslee, ed., *Constitutions of Nations,* 3rd ed. (The Hague: Martinus Nijhoff, 1966), 2:314; [United Nations], "The [Universal] Declaration of Human Rights" (1948), esp. articles 3, 6, 12, and 13, in Robert E. Sherwood, ed., *Peace on Earth* (New York: Hermitage House, 1949), 225–31.